The Samsonite Marriage:

A 40-Day Guide to God's Greatness in Your Relationship
A look into the early life of Samson before Delilah. How to make every moment in marriage monumental.

The Samsonite Marriage: A 40-Day Guide to God's Greatness in Your Relationship

Copyright © 2020 Mike Brown and Mariam Brown
Jesus in the Building Ministries

All rights reserved.

ISBN-13: 978-1-4583-2553-2

JITB Publishing | Jesus in the Building Ministries

Table of Contents

Day 1: Hindered under the hand of the enemy
Day 2: Believing in what is barren
Day 3: Voices & Visions
Day 4: Daily Discipline
Day 5: Preservation
Day 6: Preservation Part 2
Day 7: Covenant Communication
Day 8: Covenant Communication Part 2
Day 9: The Day that NEVER WAS - 2nd Corinthians 5:17
Day 10: Direct Dialogue with the Decision Maker
Day 11 Hearing the helpmate, healing the marriage
Day 12: Magnetic Pull #Run
Day 13: Slow down & let the leader lead
Day 14: Attributes of Authority
Day 15: Leading the follower
Day 16: REpeating
Day 17: Leading to serve / 'Power Couple'
Day 18: Super meets Natural
Day 19: Name Recognition 'Expect Excellence'
Day 20: The Mystery
Day 21: Sacrificial Presentation to God
Day 22: Facing The Flames
Day 23: The Power of Absolute Certainty
Day 24: Clothing The Naked Eye
Day 25: Breathing Life #CPR
Day 26: Born Blessed
Day 27: Sea of forgetfulness -Micah 7:19 KJV
Day 28: Moving by the Spirit during times of transition
Day 29: REcap
Day 30: Beauty Blinds Logic
Day 31: Crucial Conflict
Day 32: Obviously Omitted
Day 33: Unwavering Wants
Day 34: Window of Opportunity
Day 35: Ready for the Roar
Day 36: The Spirit of The Lord. It's on YOU
Day 37: Stop, Look & Listen
Day 38: Turn it around
Day 39: Full Disclosure in Marriage
Day 40: RSVP

Introduction

In our society today, there is a never-ending search for the perfect formula for creating a fabulous relationship. There are endless possibilities to obtain a promising partnership with the one that you are in love with. With so many relationships ending short of the old adage 'til death do us part,' it's time that our society takes a fresh look at some new progressive methods that will help to recalibrate relationships to a place of stability allowing them to stand the test of time. Marriage comes with many warnings about the realities regarding the many challenges that a couple will face yet it is important to remind yourself that marriage, which is the world's highest union, is to be filled with fun, friendship and fellowship with each other.

There's a saying that "laughter is good like medicine," therefore as couples mutually communicate their love it creates unity that establishes power as they move together. You can see this genuine excitement for each other as newlyweds. They are inseparable at first. They are touching, tugging and playfully pulling on each other nonstop therefore it is evident how they feel about their spouse. Even during meals at a restaurant, without respect to a special occasion, love in the air makes every moment monumental and memorable.

My wife and I are pastors but, most importantly, we are studiers of love because we have found that anything that you love you must study. We have been studying love so intensely that It has driven us to meticulously create a plan for a prosperous and productive partnership in our

The Samsonite Marriage: A 40-Day Guide to God's Greatness in Your Relationshi

upcoming book titled Protect & Polish: The Jewel In Your Crown/ A Manuscript For A Magnificent Marriage. We hope it will help to change relationships all around the world. Without delving deep into the Bible, there is one particular story that we feel demonstrates this idea of a 'Power Couple' and it is found in the Book of Judges.

The thirteenth chapter of Judges tells the story of the birth of the strongest man in the world known as Samson and it focuses in on the interactions between his parents as husband and wife. The story allows us to see Samson's father, Manoah, lead his wife by communicating a unified mindset while facing the greatest challenge of their life, which established them as a power couple on a course to connect with their covenant.

Many people recognize Michelle and Barak Obama as a power couple mainly because they are prominent people, who are faithfully pursuing their professional purpose and they have reached great heights of success. Many of our entertainment figures have become our role models with their marriages such as Denzel Washington and his wife, Paulette, because of their fame, fortune and fashionable formula that garners our attention. However, being a power couple cannot be limited to tangible success and it is not defined by professional achievements or social acceptance, instead it can be measured by one's character and the characteristics that one displays that will ultimately determine your prominence.

Manoah and his wife were leading by offering to serve the angel of the lord as a sign of appreciation for the prophetic word spoken over their lives. Great leaders are men and women who are willing to be the first to serve. Our society has seen the erosion of the spirit of meekness and the joy of servitude by being replaced by the 'satisfaction of selfishness'. The structure of family has been steadily decaying for some time now and very rarely does our community reflect the plan of family as designed by God.

Men have taken a back seat from being 'visible and vocal leaders' and women have been more 'dominant and demanding' figures in our society. The balance of power has unfortunately shifted from family purpose to fancy perceptions that promote individuality, self-reliance and self-exaltation. There are far too many people that are married living single and singles living as though they are married. Every relationship should consist of two people pursuing a common goal together with their expression of love for each otherreflecting their love.

The Samsonite Marriage: A 40-Day Guide to God's Greatness in Your Relationship

Regardless of who makes more money, who's more educated or who's the more saved, seasoned saint's marriages should reinforce UNITY. The language used should reflect the purpose of the union, therefore you should naturally hear 'we' and 'us' and very seldom should we hear individualized words such as 'I' in the daily communication of the couple. In the story of Samson, Manoah spoke to an angel on behalf of his wife said, "We would like for you to stay a while" AND "We want to cook a young goat for you to eat" and that displayed how power couples walk in unity and togetherness while being great helpmates to one another to accomplish and achieve great things together.

Rings & Things…

One of the most beautiful parts of the marriage ceremony that many love and is universally seen as the apex is the exchanging of the rings, as well as other things and I say things because in many cultures there are a vast array of items that are given as part of the wedding to show commitment and sincerity. The ring represents a flow of love, an unbroken realm of unity and oneness as the couple becomes unified in love. In John 10:30 Jesus says "I and the Father are ONE" therefore it is with that same oneness that the church becomes the bride of Christ.

A man is to love his wife as Christ loved the church and this love was shown when HE prayed for the church and taught the ways of HIS Father. Too often the wedding rings become a materialistic symbol of marriage devoid of intangible, everlasting bond for eternity. Rings have become status symbols, territorial markers but the true exchange isformed within the heart that manifest onto our hands in reverence of the Lord Jesus exchanging his life for our sins…

Christ chose to lay his life down and that is the ultimate sacrificial act that can not be undone. It is with that understanding that we should honor the covenant between husbandand wife with the exchanging of vows.

In real time, Pastor Mariam and I practice this continual exchange of the 'things of God' to help one another each and every day which strengthens our marriage. On our morningprayer line, Pastor Mariam can be heard praying for me to encourage, inspire and motivate the greatness within me. This public display of love and affection saturates the atmosphere and manifest miracles within my life and seeks to bind up dangers seen andunseen. Then I piggyback off of her prayers and speak that our marriage is filled with loving communication, unity and power and that there is a magnetic pull between us which is held together by the agape love of Christ forming a power couple that are joint heirs with God as we speak with one voice.

The Samsonite Marriage: A 40-Day Guide to God's Greatness in Your Relationsh

Watching this is action is a beautiful site and it is one that all marriages can implement into their daily lives to restore love and peace within the covenant. I encourage every couple to try it and see how your rings are no longer just on your finger; it is part of your finger. It is your finger, and nothing can undo it.

Grab your seatbelts and get ready for a journey through the early life of one of the strongest men to ever live: Samson.

Day 1: Hindered Under the Hand of the Enemy

"And the children of Israel did evil again in the sight of the Lord; and the Lord delivered them into the hand of the Philistines forty years." **Judges 13:1 KJV**

As we embark on a 40-day study into the book of Judges, Chapters 13 and 14, we will look at the remarkable life of Samson. Samson's story offers a guide that can benefit our marriages and significant relationships for generations to come. During this time, we are encouraged to examine our behaviors and challenge our thinking from a biblical perspective. The purpose is to help us reach the lofty spiritual goals we set out for our relationships. Pastor Mariam and I are excited to begin this spiritual journey with you.

To kick off our study, we will explore the complex crossroads in the Bible where the chosen people of Israel became slaves to their archenemy, the Philistines, due to past evil they had committed. Now you may be asking yourself, "what does this have to do with love, marriage, and relationships?" Trust me, I asked the same question! After meditating on the scripture for several hours, the question finally occurred to me: *how often do we overlook our past and how it impacts our present and future situations?*

Marriage is about finding the person God has intended to a joint heir, together with Christ here on Earth. But men and women often approach this process differently. Men are taught to "sow their royal oats" until the right one comes along. Women have been taught to wait for Mr. Right to come and sweep her off her feet. In a sense it is a fairytale for her. But in reality, life is a neither a never-ending conquest nor a fairytale, and it can become a nightmare if you have made decisions in your past that were not based on faith. Men, how often have things gone wrong with the so-called "right one?" Women, how about when you find out that you picked Mr. Wrong instead of Mr. Right? Sometimes those decisions can leave you with feelings of bitterness, anger, distrust and, ultimately, a lack of forgiveness. Unfortunately, we often bring unforgiveness into a marriage that only thrives when forgiveness and love are the main ingredients. The children of Israel made mistakes in their past that left them under the hand of the enemy. Today, the "enemy" we face is what keeps us from having trusted and loving relationships. We have to revisit our past to get closure on the wrongs so that we can make our marriages alright (get it: "All Right"?)

God chose a season of forty years where he dealt with the past mistakes of his own people. But very few of us have that kind of patience. Instead, we say the things like, "It's my turn," or "It's time to settle down," or even, "My biological clock is ticking." The truth is, the promises of God are not subject to our time. So we must learn to revisit our past without RE-engaging in it. Otherwise, we will find ourselves wrapped in a deeply woven web of confusion and chaos.

Marriage cannot be seen as a last resort or a last-ditch attempt at happiness. Unhealthy marriages are filled with unhappy people; people whose happiness has been undone by unrealistic expectations. God will perform His perfect work, but it requires our patience. Do not expect your marriage to change overnight. It takes time. The Bible says, *"But let patience have her perfect work, that ye may be perfect and entire, wanting nothing." James 1:4 KJV*

Reflection:
Here are some tips to help you in your relationships today:

- Old relationships are a manifestation of past decisions that stemmed from past beliefs.
- REvisit without RE-engaging. Study the wrong decisions of yesterday so that you can make the right ones today.
- Unforgiveness leaves an unforgettable memory that hinders your mind.
- Remember God's promises versus our timing. Be patient.

With love always,
Pastors Mike & Mariam Brown

The Samsonite Marriage: A 40-Day Guide to God's Greatness in Your Relationship

Day 2: **Believing in What is Barren**

"And there was a certain man of Zorah, of the family of the Danites, whose name was Manoah; and his wife was barren, and bare not." Judges 13:2

We are so happy that you are on this adventure through the scriptures. Relationships are the centerpiece of life, and as such, it is important to study how we can preserve the relationships with those that we love. Above all else, we hope that you are encouraged to work through any situations to ensure the health and vitality of all the relationships in your life. We look forward to hearing your feedback and receiving your comments as it relates to these studies.

As we take a look at the second day of our study, we are led to a powerful scripture that captures the introduction of Samson's father, Manoah. Manoah was married to a woman who, by natural standards, could not have children. There are times in our life where we are attached to things that do not seem like they will be prosperous. In these instances, it is necessary to REmind yourself, or change your perspective and REdirect your thoughts to a place where you recognize that **every moment is monumental, and our Master is miraculous.**

Step one: Recognize that every moment is monumental.

We often stay in unfruitful and nonproductive situations because we feel comfortable there. But once we realize that we are unhappy, we hit a crossroads. We begin to think that the time and energy we put in all along was meaningless. In the Bible, Manoah and his wife stayed strong in her barrenness by holding onto faith that someday their fate would change. In your own marriage, you may be charged with holding onto faith, despite when things look barren in your relationship. There are times when the arguments, fights, disagreements, and challenges seem unbearable. Your faith will help you in those moments where difficulties create a divide in your relationship.

Step two: REmind yourself that the Master is miraculous.

There are places in many marriages that require one of the partners to believe in the miraculous with the mind of the Master. When you think with the mind of the Master your whole perspective of what is barren will begin to change. Genesis says that we are 'made in HIS image and likeness' but life has a way of distracting us and manipulating our minds to minimize the Masters' miracles. Manoah was the beholder of his wife's beauty aka /ˈbyoōdē/ and he began to believe in what was barren because he was married under the covenant of God.

Never look at your barren situations with pessimism and negativity. Instead REmind yourself and add new thoughts of 'peace with an expected end' as it is said in

The Samsonite Marriage: A 40-Day Guide to God's Greatness in Your Relationship

Jeremiah 29:11. You must put on the mind of Christ and begin to see your whole world through a clearer lens. It is important to have a sanctified mind, which is having pure thoughts as well as holy and righteous intentions that will bring forth amazing results.

Let me address the term AND the bold lettering of what it means to 'REmind yourself' because it may be the proverbial 'Elephant In The Room', which by the way is a quick shoutout to Hip Hop great and Instagram inspiration Fat Joe, who had an album of the same name that spoke to the obvious things that we regularly overlook in our lives. Let's not forget that Fat Joe blessed the world with the phrase '" yesterday's price is NOT todays price" which when applied to marriage shows us that things can change from day to day.

Marcy Projects Mogul JAY-Z quoted Notorious B.I.G, Christopher Wallace on the song 'A Dream' from the Blueprint 2 album when he said "Hov' REmind yourself, nobody built like you, you designed yourself". The phrase RE means to 'go backwards, to again address with repetition, so you must rewind the clock to see who you are and what you were created to be in comparison to what you are now. You were created to have dominion, replenish and multiply in every aspect of your life.

REmind yourself of that at every fork in the road or in times where you are making crucial life choices, especially in your relationship. JAY-Z continues by saying 'I agree, I said "my one-of-a-kind self"....OMG, we must stop and give Mr. Shawn Carter his flowers...You should come into agreement with the notion that you are indeed 'one of a kind, you are an authentic original therefore you have the power to design your life and create unimaginable goals and dreams to accomplish.

To complete the lyric, it says 'I agree, **I said** "my one of kind self, get stoned every day like **Jesus did"** ... The moments when you feel you are being stoned, attacked and ridiculed embrace it by REminding yourself that an internal fortitude is being instilled and confidence is being created during these moment.

The Samsonite Marriage: A 40-Day Guide to God's Greatness in Your Relationship

As we close, recognize that every moment is monumental in your marriage. When you REmind yourself about the power of the Lord, you can handle every one of your barren situations on a daily basis.

Reflection:

- What is barren, unprofitable or unprosperous in your relationship?
- What area in your union appears meaningless?
- Are the miracles in your life minimized because of the surrounding circumstance?

With love always,
Pastors Mike & Mariam Brown

Day 3: **Voices & Visions**

"And the angel of the Lord appeared unto the woman, and said unto her: Behold now, thou art barren, and bearest not: but thou shalt conceive, and bear a son." Judges 13:3 KJV

On this third day of our joyous journey in the book of Judges, we find ourselves looking into a heavenly conversation that serves as a guide for marriage, regardless of what stage it is in. We look forward to hearing your feedback and reading your responses to these studies.

Step one: Develop a spiritual connection with heaven.

Having a strong, transparent, and spiritual connection can develop a poignant and powerful mindset in you that REdefines your destiny.

In Judges, Samson's mother is having a conversation with the "angel of the Lord," who has a miraculous message for her life. Having spiritual advisors like these are important to our marriages. When you have a strong connection with a pastor or a preacher, that advisor can help you understand the plan that God has for his people. There are times in marriage when the voice of the Lord can seem faint, confusing, or nonexistent. Do not be discouraged when you don't hear the Lord. He may be sending his word through uncommon channels to get you to tune in to him.

Step two: Avoid overreacting when the obvious is overstated.

The Lord is all-knowing and all-seeing, which allows him to see our end before we know the beginning. The angel told Manoah's wife that she was barren, which was no secret to her. But she does not overreact when the obvious truth is overstated. She remains focused and keeps her emotions in check.

Emotion destroys our devotion to our God, whose mercy endures. Oftentimes we hear things in marriage like, "you always" do this, or "I never see you" doing that. Guilt, shame and embarrassment can make us overreact towards our spouse's actions. Emotions cause us to nag the wound instead of nursing it back to total and complete healing. The Bible teaches us to forgive the mistakes, shortcomings, and issues that are obvious to us. We are asked to step higher than the obvious hindrances in our communication system.

Step three: Do not conform to controversy

In the final part of Judges, we find these words, "but thou shalt conceive, and bear a son." Not confirming the controversy is an important step that may seem impossible to do in the heat of the moment. The angel gave Manoah's wife a prophetic word that could have caused a major controversy because it went against everything that was seen in the natural.

In our marriage, we are advised to be "transformed by the renewing of your mind," according to Romans 12:1-2. Our minds should not yield to what things look like on the surface, because those things usually will not last long. You do not have to conform your own marriage to the statistics, trends or failures of previous marriages around you.

Manoah's wife faced the daunting task of hearing a controversial word that conflicted with her desires. There are times when we believe the negative and shortsighted view of our lives. Keep your eyes on what the Lord says about your life! Do be conformed to the image of this world. Marriage can only last when we leave behind the old ways, habits, and thoughts of failure and unhappiness and cleave to the covenant promise of love andunity within our relationship.

Reflection:

- On a scale of 1-10, with 10 being the highest, how would you rate your relationship with your spiritual advisor? Do you trust your advisor's voice?
- What are some obvious areas of your life that need to improve?
- Was there a time when you were conflicted about where you were versus where God said you were going?

Talk with your spouse or intended spouse about the challenges and obstacles that may be preventing your marriage from being the union that God promised. These can include work schedules, communication breakdowns, and/or financial frustrations that may cause controversy between you two.

With love always,
Pastors Mike & Mariam Brown

Day 4: **Daily Discipline**

"Now therefore beware, I pray thee, and drink not wine nor strong drink, and eat not any unclean thing." Judges 13:4 KJV

Instructions are given by the angel of the Lord to prepare for destiny. Let us look at how those instructions relate to our marriages. We look forward to hearing your feedback andreading your responses to these studies.

Step one: Having an ear to hear

Day 4 of our journey into Judges is upon us. As we continue on the march through the early life of the lineage of Samson, we find that the fourth day is a major focus on disciplineas it relates to achieving greatness.

The angel of the Lord continues his conversation with the mother of the unborn child Samson and what he says is life altering. As led by God, the angel of the Lord gives Manoah's wife some very strict instructions to watch what she put into her body. He told her to be careful because her actions would undoubtedly affect the child that she was destined to carry and subsequently birth into the world. Let's stop here and relate these instructions to marriage. It is important to be able to hear from the Lord concerning whathe has given to you to carry? Our natural instinct is lean on our thoughts and emotions regarding how to make our marriages better. There are times that we seek the advice of our friends and family which can yield mixed results. The best way to have a beautiful marriage is to hear from the Lord through the following:

- Praying without ceasing concerning important issues in your marriage
- Fasting on a regular basis to keep your natural, fleshly responses under control
- Studying the Word of God to understand the master plan for your life with your spouse.

Step two: Handle with care #Fragile

Anytime you purchase a fragile item from a store there are always instructions on how to carry the item to ensure the products safety as well as yours!! If you carry a heavy TV in the wrong manner you could hurt your back and you could drop the TV. The same goes for your marriage in that God has given each spouse a responsibility to effectively carry out their duties. There are certain instructions that the Apostle Paul gave to married couples to ensure success. Each spouse is being used by God to fulfill the needs of each other. Since the husband is the head, with Christ over him, it is his job to meet honor, respect, submit and ultimately love his wife as he loves himself because there is no other person on the earth that can fulfill that position. Likewise, the wife is to humbly do the same for her husband as unto the Lord. If a spouse refuses to meet the other spouses spiritual, emotional and natural needs there is a major void that leaves room for the enemy to invade. Manoah's wife was told that whatever she decided to eat or drink would change the destiny of her son!!!! Spouses seek to avoid the intake of things such as fear, strife, anger, silence, as well socioeconomic pressures and unfaithful desires that can negatively alter destiny.

Reflection:
Here are some tips to perfect the handing of fragile items within the marriage:

- What things or what people are you around that affect your marriage? Who are your closest friends? What are your favorite places? This will help you understand what is influencing your life.
- Setup a schedule to create discipline in your life to focus only on improving your marriage. This may mean committing to reading bible plans on marriage or biblically based books. You may also become a part of a marriage group and commit to actively participating within in it.
- Have daily prayer with your spouse before each day and at the close of every evening.

With love always,
Pastors Mike & Mariam Brown

The Samsonite Marriage: A 40-Day Guide to God's Greatness in Your Relationship

Day 5: **Preservation**

"For, lo, thou shalt conceive, and bear a son; and no razor shall come on his head: for the child shall be a Nazarite unto God from the womb: and he shall begin to deliver Israel out of the hand of the Philistines." Judges 13:5 KJV

Today is the fifth day of our interactive look into the life a great warrior for the kingdom of God and how it birthed a promise. In this two-step lesson, our goal is the understanding of preservation power. The focus will be on the *power of prevention* to preserve health in any area of your life. When we look at healthy marriages implementing systems of prevention will help defeat the decay, disease and death of the love within the couple.

Step One: Preservation of information

In the fifth verse of Judges 13, we find Samson's mother being instructed to preserve the spiritual nature of God that will soon dwell with the male child, Samson. Not to be understated it is important to note that this is second prophetic word given by the angel of the Lord confirming the birth of a son. In marriage we often see God sending HIS word multiple times to REmind us of promises that were spoken over our lives. You must actively preserve these promises by meditating on them both day and night, which is not to sit in a yoga-like state all day, but it means to be more cognizant and aware of what God has planned for your life.

Do not get consumed with your shortcomings and drawbacks that have the potential to divert you from your destiny. In marriage we must REmind ourselves, as well as our spouses, of what God has spoken over their lives and that means you will need to spend time with The Lord in prayer to understand HIS revelatory promises for your life as joint heirs with Christ.

Tips

- **Make daily confessions.** Every day, you should have a short list of purposeful points that you can speak aloud to affirm your ascension into heavenly realms of thoughts regarding your marriage.
- **Avoid daily confusions.** Steer clear of thoughts and ideas that have you pulled in opposing directions. Deny ideas that promote the stagnation of your success and delete moments of mixed emotions. For example, *"I love my spouse, but I hate when they always do this..."*

Step Two: Activation of information is vital to victory

The second level of today's lesson is the activation of the information that has been given to you is *vital to victory!* Our faith needs to be activated, which is to make the word became flesh or tangible in our lives. Samson's mother had to let the word marinate in her mind yet there needed to be the moment that her faith manifested into works. The Bible says that Samson would be born as a Nazarite, which is one who is separated to serve God in life and lifestyle. Many times, we are married but our lifestyle does not reflect the life that we vowed to live. Healthy marriages need to have a unified mission, mutually beneficial blessings and freedom from all familiar foundations of the past.

Samson was going to be used by God to bring deliverance to a captive people because he was destined to be great from birth. He was the best weapon that God had to conquer the enemies of the kingdom of God. Realize that in your marriage you are being used as an instrument of God to intimidate the enemy that is trying to invade your relationship. Activate your mind and accept the challenge to usher in changes that will cause your marriage to flourish. Despite being barren at one point in her life, Samson's mother was birthing the best that God had to offer!

Reflection:

- Construct a short list of challenges in your marriage, in terms of you and your spouse believing what you are birthing is the best that God has to

offer.
- Create a list of special skills, talents and abilities that you feel can maximize your marital potential.
- Activate an area of your faith in these special realms and document how you see it changing your marriage for the better. Document all results.

With love always,
Pastors Mike & Mariam Brown

Day 6: Preservation Part II

"For, lo, thou shalt conceive, and bear a son; and no razor shall come on his head: for the child shall be a Nazarite unto God from the womb: and he shall begin to deliver Israel out of the hand of the Philistines." Judges 13:5 KJV

In medicine, they say that prevention is the best medicine. The easiest mess to cleanup, is a mess that never happened. We hope that you gain some valuable perspective from this lesson and we look forward to hearing your feedback and receiving your comments as it relates to these studies.

Step Two: Activation of information is vital to victory

Today's lesson is the second level of the activation. Together with level one, the information presented here is vital to your victory! Our faith needs to be activated, which is to make the Word became flesh or tangible in our lives. Samson's mother had to let the Word marinate in her mind yet there needed to be the moment that her faith manifested into works. The Bible says that Samson would be born as a Nazarite, which is one who is separated to serve God in life and lifestyle. Many times we are married, but our lifestyle does not reflect the life that we vowed to live. Healthy marriages need to have a unified mission, mutually beneficial blessings and freedom from familiar foundations of the past.

Samson was going to be used by God to bring deliverance to a captive people because he was destined to be great from birth. He was created to be a formidable weapon that God would use to conquer the enemies of the kingdom of Heaven. Realize that in your marriage you are being used as an instrument of God to intimidate the enemy that is trying to invade your relationship. In fact, the bible tells us in 2 Corinthians 5:20 that we are "ambassadors of Christ." Activate your mind and accept the challenge to usher in changes that will cause your marriage to flourish. Despite being barren at one point in her life, Samson's mother was birthing the best that God had to offer!

Reflection:

- Construct a short list of challenges in your marriage, in terms of you and yourspouse believing what you are birthing is the best that God has to offer.
- Create a list of special skills, talents and abilities that you feel can maximize yourmarital potential. Activate.

With love always,
Pastors Mike & Mariam Brown

Day 7: Covenant Communication

On this seventh day of our journey, we find the initial interaction between Manoah and his wife and this conversation is rooted in meekness which is a key element in what I call covenant communication, which is how individuals that are guided by God should communicate with one another.

"Then the woman came and told her husband, saying, A man of God came unto me, and his countenance was like the countenance of an angel of God, very terrible: but I asked him not whence he was, neither told he me his name:"
Judges 13:6 KJV

Step One: Heavenly Help

There is a strong relationship between heaven and earth in terms of God's will to be donehere in the natural realm. In the Lord's Prayer Christ teaches the disciples to pray in a manner that is very simple, yet it yields tremendous power. Manoah's wife has an amazing encounter with an angel of the Lord that awakens her spiritual ears to hear the promise of God over her life. This angelic figure was mind blowing but it is what Manoah's wife does upon hearing him that amazes me. After hearing the word that she will go from barren to birthing, Manoah's wife immediately seeks out her husband to share the wonderful news. It is important that we keep our communication consistent within the covenant of God because it is the most sacred relationship on earth. Your spouse should be the first to know when something significant occurs in your life. The powers of heaven are manifested in our life to drive us to communicate a joint covenant effectively towards one another.

Too often spouses are the last to know when you're happy, sad, angry, blessed or whatever emotion you are experiencing throughout your day. It is unfortunate that the coworkers know before the spouse, the girlfriends are confided in before the husband or the fellas know about the plans before the wife. We must keep all communication within the confines of the covenant. This is not gender specific, but it is important that we address this immediately!!! Try and make your spouse your first call in ALL THINGS! If you seek out counsel or validation before communicating with your spouse, you are endangering your covenant by violating the sacred nature of your marriage.

Reflection:

- Discuss your daily agenda or itinerary with your spouse prior to your day.

The Samsonite Marriage: A 40-Day Guide to God's Greatness in Your Relationship

- Notify your spouse of any unexpected changes, delays or alterations in your day that might cause a disruption in your spirit.
- Pray before you lay down at night to provide closure to these potentially toxic elements within your life.

With love always,
Pastors Mike & Mariam Brown

Day 8: Covenant Communication (Part II)

"Then the woman came and told her husband, saying, A man of God came unto me, and his countenance was like the countenance of an angel of God, very terrible: but I asked him not whence he was, neither told he me his name:" Judges 13:6 KJV

On this eighth day of our journey we find that there is an expectation of excellency of the power of God to be performed in the horizontal realm. As a recap of Day Seven, we witnessed the initial interaction between Manoah and his wife. This conversation is rooted in meekness which is a key element in what I call covenant communication. This is how individuals that are guided by God should communicate with one another. We look forward to hearing your feedback and receiving your comments as it relates to these studies.

Step one: Practice Meekness

In part two of Covenant Communication, our study allows us to see a woman working in the wisdom of God by demonstrating humility, meekness and submission unto the Word of The Lord as well as her husband. Our society shuns humility and other godly attributes that resemble love because it is felt that if we are vulnerable then we will be violated. God tells us in the fifth chapter of Matthew that the "meek shall inherit the earth" and you have to REmind yourself that being MEEK DOES NOT MAKE YOU WEAK!

Manoah's wife was given the charge that she was about to do some heroic things here in the horizontal realm. Two things were important for this miracle to come forth in their lives:

- Manoah's wife had to be meek to receive the word from the man of God
- Manoah had to be meek to allow his wife to express her experiences to him without discouraging this heavenly encounter

It was spoken over her life that she was going from barren to birthing a mighty king! I feel like preaching. Ladies, you can go from being stressed to being blessed in a heartbeat. Men, with one change of thought, you can go from being down and out to saying NOTHING CAN STOP ME I'M ALL THE WAY UP! It is important that you know who you are in the eyes of your Father. You are HIS HERO and HE expects HEROICS in this horizontal place that we call home. Let the church say AMEN!

Manoah's wife became a HEROINE for the children of Israel and her husband became an instant HERO and together they were about to perform the greatest feat EVER known to God's people at that time. When husband and wife recognize the power that they have by walking in one accord it is a changemaker and a game changer.

Without meekness, which is a form of love, you cannot expect to inherit the things thathave been laid up for you through the death of Christ

Reflection:

- Allow the word of the Lord to pierce your heart so that the heroics that are trappedinside of you can come to fruition inside of your relationships
- Discuss the plans that The Lord is placing over your marriage
- Trust in the Lord to speak through HIS vessels to help facilitate a unified marchinto the realm of the miraculous within your marriage.
- Interact with your spouse on who is in their trusted inner circle. It should includespiritually minded individuals that want to see your union thrive.

With love always,
Pastors Mike & Mariam Brown

The Samsonite Marriage: A 40-Day Guide to God's Greatness in Your Relationship

Day 9: The Day That Never Was – II Corinthians 5:17

You are a New Creature, bury your mistakes

Reflection Day

Day 10: Direct Dialogue with the Decision Maker

"Then Manoah entreated the Lord, and said, O my Lord, let the man of God which thou didst send come again unto us, and teach us what we shall do unto the child that shall be born." Judges 13:8 KJV

Additional Scriptural Reference for God being the decision-maker over your destiny:

"Looking unto Jesus the author and finisher of our faith; who for the joy that was set before him endured the cross, despising the shame, and is set down at the right hand of the throne of God." Hebrews 12:2 KJV

On this wonderful journey into the book of Judges, our Day 10 text allows us to hear Manoah's voice for the very first time and he begins to dialogue with the ONE who controls destiny. Manoah asked God for another visitation from the angel that carried a word of victory for their marriage!!! It is important to expect victory in your marriage and reject all presumptions of defeat. When you speak with God it is key that you know that HE is the decision-maker who has the final say. We look forward to your feedback and comments regarding this study.

Position yourself to receive your blessing by having daily dialogues with God and HIS WORD. You can control the destiny of your marriage when you are not afraid to embrace what God has planned for you and your marriage. Engage God regarding the direction that you and your spouse should be going. The Lord will provide revelation with clarity and the picture of your marriage will develop in hi-definition precision.

Many times, the enemy causes us to be fearful and timid, in areas of our marriage that require faith. It takes faith to express love, forgiveness, humility and submission to your spouse. Operating in love, as well as the other fruits of the spirit, are without a doubt very difficult to master, with the natural mind, but I urge you to remember that Christ gives you the power to 'quench all the fiery darts of the wicked'. Having daily dialogues with God will provide a covenant confidence that the most difficult things become more attainable with God.

Married couples, it is paramount that you press towards the mark of the high calling given by God. Remember that the steps of a good man or woman are ordered by God. If your marriage is not being led by the Lord who is the one who is to guide us through dark moments that needs to be changed. Manoah's faith to speak with God is what we can model our lives after.

Reflection:

- Create a list of things in your marriage that you need to discuss with God
- Write down what you think God would say to you about your questions
- Ask your spouse what they need from God and what do they need from you, interms of prayer and encouragement

Begin to pray as a couple for all of the questions, topics of concern and areas ofopportunity in your marriage.

With love always,
Pastors Mike & Mariam Brown

Day 11: **Hearing the Helpmate, Healing the Marriage**

And God hearkened to the voice of Manoah; and the angel of God came again untothe woman as she sat in the field: but Manoah her husband was not with her." Judges 13:9 KJV

On this eleventh day of our journey into the life and times of Samson, we find one of the most important things needed in a healthy, spiritual marriage which is to have a magnetic pull towards one another! In our previous day Manoah's wife was in a position to 'sit andsmile' while The Lord was sending a word of confirmation on their destiny. Now we find the wife receiving everything that her husband prayed for and the moment she received confirmation she ran to her husband which represented a magnetic pull. We look forward to your comments and feedback about the study content and scriptures.

God heard the voice of Manoah as he petitioned The Lord to send the angel to confirm the instructions on how to raise the unborn Samson. Manoah speaks to God but his wifegets the visitation from the angel. An interesting point that is made in this scripture, is when you speak to God you also have to trust that you HE hears you.

Today one of the most frustrating things is feeling like you are not being heard. Manoah's wife was in perfect position to receive the messenger of the Lord. In this passage Manoah's wife was the perfect helpmate in the relationship because she waitedpatiently as God answered her husband's prayers. You and your spouse are a dynamic duo daringly driving through life's obstacle course towards your destiny. Every person plays an important role in the success of the marriage. Manoah spoke with God andtrusted that he was being heard and his wife had to 'sit and smile' until she receivedconfirmation from God.

In marriage there are times when miscommunication disrupts the unity and power that is generated by love. A key point in any significant relationship is remembering that you come from two totally separate ways of life only to be merged together with minimal counseling on godly communication skills. Because you are learning on the job it is normal that you will make some mistakes along the way. Do not get discouraged or get down onyourself as a result of your mistakes, instead encourage yourself to find resolutions for allissues in your life.

The enemy is a specialist at causing division within a union that is predestined to be indivisible! Be comfortable with your role in the marriage and appreciate the position that your spouse holds as well because it takes two to make a thing go right!!! As we close out this portion of our study let's look at the original plan for marriage right out of the mouth of Jesus. "But from the beginning of the creation God made them male and female. For

The Samsonite Marriage: A 40-Day Guide to God's Greatness in Your Relationship

this cause shall a man leave his father and mother, and cleave to his wife; And they twain shall be one flesh: so then they are no more twain, but one flesh. What therefore God hath joined together, let not man put asunder (Mark 10:6-9 KJV)."

Reflection:

- Think of a time when you prayed for a situation and your spouse saw it come to pass before you did.
- What is your role, as a spirit-led individual, within the marriage?
- Are you comfortable with role that you are playing or have played in your marriage?

Things are moving while you are sitting still.

With love always,
Pastors Mike & Mariam Brown

Day 12: **Magnetic Pull #Run**

"And the woman made haste, and ran, and shewed her husband, and said unto him, Behold, the man hath appeared unto me, that came unto me the other day." **Judges 13:10 KJV**

<u>**Additional Scripture Reference**</u>: "What therefore God hath joined together, let not man put asunder." Mark 10:9 KJV

In every relationship there must be a supernatural force, which is the love of God, shared by two individuals that defy gravity in pulling them together. In your relationship there can be NOTHING that stops you from being drawn to your spouse and sharing the most important and intimate moments with each other. "What therefore God hath joined together, let not man put asunder." Mark 10:9 KJV

Life presents many challenges such as work schedules, parental obligations and social commitments that create a tug of war scenario that ultimately creates divisions within the marriage. The scripture speaks on work schedules to the point that one will eat and break bread as a reward for what has been worked for with godly conduct. The Lord wants balance in every area of our lives so the unity of our marriages will not be disrupted. "For even when we were with you, this we commanded you, that if any would not work, neither should he eat." 2 Thessalonians 3:10 KJV

The word of God continues teaching on spiritual balance while working by saying "Now them that are such we command and exhort by our Lord Jesus Christ, that with quietness they work, and eat their own bread."2 Thessalonians 3:12 KJV.

Quality time is one of the five love languages (which we will REintroduce) and it triggers the other four which are words of affirmation, physical touch, acts of service and presentation of special gifts towards one another. Manoah's wife ran towards her husband with a renewed vigor and an undeniable excitement about their future. There are undoubtedly things that are keeping you from spending quality time with your spouse and those issues subsequently cause the other important areas requiring love to become stagnant. The more stagnant the love is, there will be an impasse within the marriage. Start running towards your spouse with every important idea and intimate issue concerning the direction of your marriage. Try one or all of these exercises in excellence, to strive towards perfection, no matter how seemingly elusive it is for your flesh, a willingheart is God's workshop.

Exercises in Excellence:

- Stand in front of your spouse and take a step towards each other while quoting ascripture that each of you are standing.
- Exchange scriptures as vows that each of you will commit to live by.
- Find three scriptures that focus on unity within the family.

Reflection:
Our tip of the day is a scripture. The one special ingredient, the "secret sauce," to supportthat magnetic pull: *"Pray without ceasing." 1 Thessalonians 5:17 KJV*

With love always,
Pastors Mike & Mariam Brown

Day 13: Slow Down and Let the Leader Lead

"Then Manoah arose and followed his wife, and when he came to the man he said to him, "Are you the man who spoke to the woman?" And he said, "I am." Judges 13:11 NASB**

The thirteenth day of our study shows two individuals operating in unison as one entity pursuing a joint destiny. Manoah's wife had an extraordinary encounter with the man of God, also known as the angel of the lord that revealed the promise of a baby out of a barren womb. He then began to follow his wife to find the man who spoke these miracles over their family. A key point for every individual is you need to be willing to humble yourself to be led into unfamiliar territory. Every great leader was a great follower. David said that a 'righteous man's steps are ordered by the Lord' therefore each and every decision that we make should include God.

As we study this encounter, we see that obedience is a key ingredient to greatness. Too often relationships consist of two people that are legally married BUT living single. Couples make decisions without consulting one another and it leads to a divided home. Paul teaches that we need to be led by the spirit of God and ultimately remain faithful and obedient to HIS WORD to gain our everlasting freedom. Communication is the key to creating a unified position of faith.

"But if you are led by the Spirit, you are not under the Law." Galatians 5:18 NASB

At the time that Manoah's wife leads him to the man of God, Manoah is preparing to take his proper leadership role in the future of the family. Manoah asks questions of the man of God and his wife patiently waits for her husband to discern their next move. How many times are we too impatient for our blessings to come forth? Too often we cannot guard our tongue while someone else takes the lead. There's a song called 'Follow the Leader' by Eric B & Rakim that says 'no need to speed slow down and let the leader lead' and that is what we see in healthy relationships, people who are not afraid to follow the leader.

Reflection:

- Find three people that you would follow on their life missions, goals or dreams
- Why would you follow them?
- How is your life being led by God?

With love always,
Pastors Mike & Mariam Brown

Day 14: **Attributes of Authority**

So Manoah asked him, "When your words are fulfilled, what is to be the rule that governs the boy's life and work?" Judges 13:12 NIV

Our tour through the life of Samson brings us to the fourteenth day and we find some great attributes of authority that are paramount to effective leadership. Our previous focus was 'letting the leader lead' and if we reflect on the text Manoah asked, was the angel, the man of God who spoke to his wife.

The angel of the Lord answered, "I am." We will look into a few keys to greatness
within the covenant of God through Christ that need to come to the forefront of our thinking to help us understand who is the leader and why we hope you are enjoying these lessons. We love sending them to you. Our great hope is that your marriages increase in the fruits of the spirit and your understanding of love emboldens you to service. We look forward to your feedback.

Covenant Character, which is the demonstration of a divine nature dwelling in a man or woman that communicates Christ-like standards that are easily recognizable within their daily interactions.

When we see those words '*I am*' in the Bible it represents the unquestionable, undeniable and unmistakable power of God manifested in the natural realm. The angel said '*I am*' and Manoah nor his wife ever questioned the position or power of the leader, mainly because they trusted that the angel was being sent, led and instructed by The Lord.

Manoah began to interact with the angel by demonstrating the covenant characteristic of *'humility'* by asking what needs to be done to raise the miracle child, Samson. Leaders display humility as a sign of power. Leaders are quick to listen and are able to be instructed. Too often men and women have power struggles in the home because we are taught that 'loudest voice' or 'the most abrasive and aggressive' person is fit to lead.

As followers of Christ, being led by the Holy Spirit, we must recognize the power of humility as an attribute of authority. Manoah remained humble yet he was leading his family by inquiring in the things of God. His wife never spoke out of turn and she never overstepped her husband. They both remained unified in their humility and understood that they were being used by God to bring forth greatness out of their lineage.

Aggression leads to regression in the relationship. Any senseless argument could distort their destiny by causing division within the marriage. The Apostle Paul teaches this concept in the following scripture, "Do all things without grumbling or disputing; so that

The Samsonite Marriage: A 40-Day Guide to God's Greatness in Your Relationshi

you will prove yourselves to be blameless and innocent, children of God above reproach in the midst of a crooked and perverse generation, among whom you appear as lights inthe world (Philippians 2:14-15 NASB)."

With love always,
Pastors Mike & Mariam Brown

Day 15: **Leading the Follower**

So the angel of the LORD said to Manoah, "Let the woman pay attention to all that I said." Judges 13:13 NASB

Today's text has Manoah listening to the angel of the Lord giving divine instructions to him regarding God's designed course of destiny for their lives. The angel tells Manoah to 'let the woman pay attention to all that I said' and it is here that I will tap into our subject which is *'leading the follower'*. It is important to understand that every leader is first a great follower. Leaders cannot lead themselves and kings or queens are unable to crown themselves. Husbands and wives are to follow the plan of God for family. Too often our families take on roles that are outside of the designed plans of God. We pray that your families are studying these scriptures together. A family that prays together, stays together! We look forward to your feedback and welcome your comments or questions.

The Lord has laid out guidelines that will ensure greatness in the home; if it is followed by each member of the family. Paul teaches us in Corinthians about divine order in the home as it is ordained by God. There is the powerful *'let'* in the instructions provided by the angel and the word *'let'* is the same when God spoke to the universe for the first time, in the midst of darkness and said *"let there be light"*. The word *'let'* represents an authority and dominion given by God to implement HIS will in our lives. Manoah had a choice to allow the will of God to be the dominant force in his life and as a man being led by God, he chose to listen to the Lord. Leading by listening allows you to lead the follower. Manoah's wife was following him and she honored him as he took instructions from God through the angel. Trust and believe that there is power that is given unto you when you follow someone with great power!

God's plan is that every home would be led by a man who is being governed and guided by Christ, who is led by the Almighty God Himself. Paul teaches that we are a reflection of who we follow:

"Be imitators of me, just as I also am of Christ. Now I praise you because you remember me in everything and hold firmly to the traditions, just as I delivered them to you. But I want you to understand that Christ is the head of every man, and the man is the head of a woman, and God is the head of Christ." **1 Corinthians 11:1-3 NASB**

Paul's Instructions for Family Structure:

- "*Be imitators of me,*" When Paul says this, he is calling for us to do as he has done. The late Notorious BIG said "If I go? You got to go!" You are to follow the

- leader that is leading you as they are led by God and allow yourself to be a disciple. Being a disciple means you should have a strong spirit of discipline. It isimportant to be a disciple in fellowship, breaking of bread which is unity and dedicated to the teachings of the ways of Christ.

- "Just as I am of Christ," tells us that Paul sought to think, act and get results as Christ did. There is greatness in your DNA because you are made in the imageand likeness of God. Follow the blueprint given to be blessed, which is found inMatthew 5.

- "Remember me in everything and hold firmly to the traditions," which is to have amentor and model that marks the path, if and when we drift out of our lane. Haveguidelines and governors to control the speed at which you travel in your life. U- Haul moving trucks have a maximum speed and the vehicles will not go over thatspeed as a safety precaution. Stand on the word of the Lord and trust Him to keep you on the path to your destiny.

With love always,
Pastors Mike & Mariam Brown

Day 16: REpeating the message to receive the reward

"She should not eat anything that comes from the vine nor drink wine or strong drink, nor eat any unclean thing; let her observe all that I commanded." Judges 13:14 NASB

As we embark on the sixteenth day of our study in the Judges 13 it is clear that God is REpeating the message that HE wants us to receive and that message is to observe HIS commandments. There are many commandments that were given by God and we are expected to observe all of them. Being obedient to the Word of God is a key factor in inviting the omnipresent spirit of The Lord in your life. Marriage is about a man and a woman entering into a covenant with The Lord and expressing that love towards one another as they love God, who is at the center of the union. My wife and I are grateful that you are all on this journey with us. We look forward to your feedback or comments.

Manoah's wife was required to obey every word given and her husband was to be a "*pusher*" and an encouraging presence that invokes an intertwining grip onto the greatness that is planned over the couple. Husband and wife are meant to be joint heirs with Christ as they walk in unity. The angel of the Lord kept repeating the instructions that needed to be followed in order for God's plan to unfold. Couples are to complement each other as helpers along the path of righteousness. In marriage take time to complement each other and point out each other's best characteristics and to highlight those features that caused you to fall in love. There is nothing like hearing how much you areappreciated and loved by your spouse.

It is important to fight through the fleshly moments and REmind yourself to REpeat the wonderfully, blessed attributes of your spouse. Your tongue has the power to call those things that be not as though they are!! Speak that your marriage is one full of love, affection, goodness, gentleness, forgiveness, patience and every fruit of the spirit that willcause your relationship to be fruitful unto the multiplication of the blessings of the Lord that maketh one rich without adding sorrow.

REpeat this exercise:

- I am rich in love
- I am rich in joy
- I am rich in peace
- I am rich in (add your own words)
- I am rich in (add your own words)
- I am rich in (add your own words)

The Samsonite Marriage: A 40-Day Guide to God's Greatness in Your Relationship

"It is the blessing of the LORD that makes rich, And He adds no sorrow to it." Proverbs 10:22 NASB

Jesus spent plenty of time speaking life into HIS disciples and followers even when he could have been frustrated with their actions. In Luke 22 the disciples argued about who would betray Christ, yet he still spoke greatness and kingdom authority over their lives.

"You are those who have stood by Me in My trials; and just as My Father has
granted Me a kingdom, I grant you that you may eat and drink at My table in My kingdom, and you will sit on thrones judging the twelve tribes of Israel." Luke 22:28-30 NASB

Soundtrack to REmind you of your destiny:
https://www.youtube.com/shared?ci=oGY0PhIbhuw

With love always,
Pastors Mike & Mariam Brown

Day 17: **Leading to Serve #The Power Couple**

Then Manoah said to the angel of the Lord, "We would like for you to stay a while. We want to cook a young goat for you to eat." Judges 13:15 ERV

Day 17 allows us to see the Manoah led his family by communicating a unified mindset of him and his wife, which established them as a power couple on a collision course with their covenant. Many people recognize Michelle and Barack Obama as a power couple mainly because they are prominent people faithfully pursuing their professional purpose and they have reached great heights of success. Nonetheless, biblical manhood and womanhood are not defined by professional achievements or social acceptance, instead, it can be measured by the characteristics of Christ that one displays that will determine your prominence.

Manoah and his wife were leading by offering to serve the angel of the lord as a sign of appreciation for the prophetic word spoken over their lives. Great leaders are men and women who are willing to be the first to serve. Our society has seen the erosion of the spirit of meekness and the joy of servitude being replaced by the *'satisfaction of selfishness'*. The structure of family has been steadily decaying for some time now and very rarely does our community reflect the plan of the family as designed by God. Men have taken a back seat from being *'visible and vocal leaders'* and women have been more *'dominant and demanding'* figures in our society. The balance of power has unfortunately shifted from family purpose to fancy perceptions that promote **individuality, self- reliance, and self-exaltation**. There are far too many people that are married living single and singles living as though they are married.

Every relationship should consist of two people pursuing God together with their expression of love for each other reflecting their love for God. Manoah and his wife were jointly ready to serve. That message was clearly stated publicly by the head of the home and it reinforced the private agreement between the husband and the wife. Regardless of who makes more money, who's more educated or who's the more saved, seasoned saint Christian marriages should reinforce UNITY. Marriage is about being joint heirs with Christ so the language used should reflect the purpose of the union and therefore we would naturally hear 'we' and very seldom 'I' in the daily communication of the couple. Manoah said, "We would like for you to stay a while," and "We want to cook a young goat for you to eat." (Judges 13:15 ERV)

Real power couples walk in unity, being great helpmates to one another.

Reflection:

- Speak terms that signify unity i.e. "We, us, our, ours"
- Avoid terms that signify disunity i.e. "I, me, mine, yours"

With love always,
Pastors Mike & Mariam Brown

Day 18: **Super Meets the Natural**

"And the angel of the Lord said unto Manoah, Though thou detain me, I will not eat of thy bread: and if thou wilt offer a burnt-offering, thou must offer it unto the Lord. For Manoah knew not that he was an angel of the Lord." **Judges 13:16 KJV**

Today we will explore how the supernatural realm meets the natural realm within a covenant. The angel of the Lord expressed that even though he was being offered things in the tangible realm those things could not satisfy the divine appetite. As one who is spiritual, your thirst should be on the things of God because God cannot be pleased through anything fleshly.

Each individual, within the covenant, is to maintain direct communication with the Lord and practice pleasing HIM by living in the spirit by avoiding the natural desire to accommodate the flesh. The Bible says, *"Blessed are they which do hunger and thirst after righteousness: for they shall be filled."* Matthew 5:6 KJV

Manoah was able to detain and keep the attention of the angel, yet he was told that the angel was in this world but was not from it. During your communication with your spouse, it is important to resemble and reflect the heavenly world from which you were birthed. Your true citizenship is the kingdom of God in Christ. Oftentimes we try and sell supernatural issues using natural resources and remedies. Every issue in your marriage is solved by seeking the kingdom of Heaven first and foremost. Here's a scriptural reference to help you lean on God:

"For the Gentiles eagerly seek all these things; for your heavenly Father knows that you need all these things. But seek first His kingdom and His righteousness, and all these things will be added to you. So do not worry about tomorrow; for tomorrow will care for itself. Each day has enough trouble of its own." Matthew 6:32-34 NASB

It is unfortunate that couples mask problems and put bandages on ulcers which creates spiritual infections within the covenant. There are times when families argue and have disagreements that never receive closure in the natural realm. Many marriages only reconcile mentally and very rarely will they verbally express the desire to reconcile. The easy way out of a problem is to *'kiss and make up'* yet there should be clear, concise, andconsistent conversations to create change. Some say *'make up sex'* is good for relationships however sex will never solve a problem in your marriage. Seek spiritual intimacy which drives you to remain humble, while walking in love and having a heart of forgiveness and repentance. These aforementioned elements are keys to solving issues in yourlife.

The Samsonite Marriage: A 40-Day Guide to God's Greatness in Your Relationship

Reflection:

- Create a list of things that you do to please God.
- What could you add to your list that God would be pleased with?
- How does your life reflect the kingdom of God?

With love always,
Pastors Mike & Mariam Brown

Day 19: **Name Recognition #Expect Excellence**

Manoah said to the angel of the LORD, "What is your name, so that when your words come to pass, we may honor you?" Judges 13:17 NASB

As we look into our focus scripture this nineteenth day of the study on 'A Samsonite Marriage' it is important that you understand the power of name recognition in regards to honoring the covenant of marriage. The scripture begins with the mighty man Manoah who is conversing with the angel of the LORD and asks for the angel's name. Manoah had an expectation of excellence by a miracle that would come to pass through the word of the angel and since Manoah, was a man of honor he wanted to give proper honor to the angel of the LORD at the manifestation of God's word coming to pass. In marriage, God has joined two formerly independent individuals and has joined them to forever be one under one name. Marriage is about uniting the two and making them an entity that will glorify the Lord together.

When God created marriage, it was HIS expectation that the covenant union would multiply and produce great fruit. God has never planned for marriage to fail; in fact, HIS WORD provides a solution to every imaginable problem that may occur. Marriage is to be full of great expectations of miracles, signs and wonders. There are statistics that highlight the demise of marriage and the general pessimistic perceptions placed on the sustainable success of covenant relationships in our society; however, people of faith are to have an expectation of excellence.

The Samsonite Marriage: A 40-Day Guide to God's Greatness in Your Relationship

There are a few steps that will help you have an expectation of excellence within your marriage that can be found in the teachings of Christ as it pertains to what each person should exemplify in the relationship. Let's look into the fifth chapter of Matthew 5:5-10 ERV:

- BE humble, as it is a direct link to you losing the promises of God. You can expectan overflow when you have the faith to expect the best to happen for you. Great blessings belong to those who are humble. They will be given the land God promised.

- BE Righteous because our Lord is holy and righteous and HE can only dwell within a righteous man or woman. Unrighteousness removes the presence of the Lord from your life and your marriage. When you are upright before God it will satisfy every need and desire in your life. Great blessings belong to those who want to doright more than anything else. God will fully satisfy them.

- BE merciful because Gods mercy endures forever in our lives. We are to extend the same message of mercy to those in our lives. When your spouse makes a mistake, have mercy and forgive them as they have shown you mercy and forgiveness. Great blessings belong to those who show mercy to others. Mercy will be given to them. Great blessings belong to those whose thoughts are pure. They will be with God.

- BE peaceful as that is one of the characteristics of Christ. He is the prince of peace. God seeks to remove all strife and confusion from your marriage. Seek peace and pursue it. Great blessings belong to those who work to bring peace. God will call them his sons and daughters.

- BE the sufferer which is to gladly endure your trials and tribulations as a good and faithful soldier. You may face hurt feelings and mixed emotions in marriage yet you have to press through and seek the face of God to be your present help in those times of trouble. Seek God, seek wise counsel and seek prayer as these are steps towards greatness. Great blessings belong to those who suffer persecution for doing what is right. God's kingdom belongs to them.

With love always,
Pastors Mike & Mariam Brown

Day 20: **The Mystery**

He replied, "Why do you ask my name? It is beyond understanding." Judges 13:18NIV

On this twentieth day of our study we communicate our thankfulness to each other for all of the things that we experience together that positively affect our lives. Manoah was anxious to learn the name of the angel of the Lord so he and his wife could honor and bless him. An important key to marriage is each individual should be anxious to seek a higher understanding from God. The Apostle Paul teaches on marriage being a very uniquely mysterious event meant to promote the dominion, power and kingdom authority planned before the foundation of the world.

Here's a snapshot of how marriage is seen from a biblical perspective:

"This is a profound mystery—but I am talking about Christ and the church. However, each one of you also must love his wife as he loves himself, and the wife must respect her husband." Ephesians 5:32-33 NIV

Marriage is to be made up of two God-fearing individuals that hunger and thirst after righteousness. There are times when couples find themselves unequally yoked and that can be the beginning of a rocky road. Couples should have a common ground and be likeminded in their faith because there will be problems and issues that arise in the relationship. When life detours your marriage, having a common faith helps you quickly RELocate a common ground as you implement the problem-solving strategies provided by the word of God. In the twelfth chapter of Romans it says, *"Rejoicing in hope; patient in tribulation; continuing instant in prayer."* Romans 12:12 KJV

Rejoicing in hope, which is to celebrate the chance to walk by faith and not by sight, with the knowledge that God will never fail you. Take time every day to share a few joyous moments with your spouse that requires faith. Then touch and agree in prayer on those areas in your life.

Patient in tribulations which is to patiently endure the tough times knowing that God will provide his rod and staff as helpers during the dark moments. Reinforcing your commitment to each other on a daily basis is key. Remember, women need to feel the husband will provide security and men need to know that the wife believes in him.

Reflection:

- Continue in prayer, which is to handle everything with prayer.

The Samsonite Marriage: A 40-Day Guide to God's Greatness in Your Relationship

- Prayer can be 3-4 times a day, by phone, text messages and emails. It isimportant to let your spouse know that you are praying for them.
- Also ask for prayer in areas of your life that you need God to bless.

With love always,
Pastors Mike & Mariam Brown

Day 21: **Sacrificial Presentation to God**

Then Manoah took a young goat, together with the grain offering, and sacrificed it on a rock to the Lord. And the Lord did an amazing thing while Manoah and his wife watched. Judges 13:19 NIV

On this 21st day of our study on *The Samsonite Marriage* we will dive into the manifestation of the prophetic promises that were made unto Manoah and his wife and was ushered in by the sacrificial offering unto God. He and his wife offered a pure, unblemished young goat as an offering of thanksgiving and appreciation for the promise of God coming forth. Marriage can be measured by the amount of sacrifices that each spouse is willing to offer up to make the relationship prosperous. A union designed by God, to reach perfection, has to incorporate the death or dying off of something before new life can be birthed.

Each member of the relationship will be defined by their willingness to present parts of their life to God, as a sacrifice to prevent any potential hindrances that are harmful to the marriage. Some examples of hindrances to marriages are old relationships, unresolved hurts and disappointments as well as third party members, such as family, friends, coworkers and even social media that influence the marriage in some way. The Bible, in Genesis 2:24-26 talks about men and women leaving everything in their past to cleave unto their spouse, which means husbands and wives need to relinquish ALL PAST

The Samsonite Marriage: A 40-Day Guide to God's Greatness in Your Relationship

ATTACHMENTS AND AFFILIATIONS with their former lives. Manoah and his wife wanted to please God, therefore they offered the sacrifice and enjoyed how it would please God. If you are struggling to give up anything from your former lifestyle you are endangering the health of the marriage. There are times that couples struggle leaving old boyfriends and girlfriends in the past and they bring the old baggage into their present and future life. Couples, I urge you to distance yourself from your past and present your life as a living sacrifice that is holy and acceptable unto God

Reflection:

- Create a list of things that may be present in your marriage that is from your past. This can be a list of old partners, gifts, pictures, clothing, bags, and lingerie
- Create a list of things that you would like you and your partner to present to God that creates a unified position within the marriage.
- Implement strategic prayer for the lists that you and your spouse have created.

With love always,
Pastors Mike & Mariam Brown

Day 22: **Facing the Flames**

For it came about when the flame went up from the altar toward heaven, that the angel of the LORD ascended in the flame of the altar. When Manoah and his wife saw this, they fell on their faces to the ground. Judges 13:20 NASB

As we embark on the 22nd day of our extensive study of the characteristics of a 'Samsonite Marriage' we find Manoah and his wife falling in the face of the flames that represent the miraculous sign from the Lord. The offering that was made by Manoah and his wife sparked the amazing ascension of the angel. When spouses stand in unity and offer things up to God it provokes a divine response from heaven. When you stand in unity it blesses God because the bible emphasizes the power of two dwelling on one accord. Every decision that is made in your home, whether small or large, requires both parties to be in agreement. There will be times in your marriage where it is under attack but you must withstand every fiery dart of the enemy. Resist the temptation to quit or walkout, instead fall down on your face and seek the Lord for answers. God will hear from heaven and heal your land on which your marriage rests when you humble yourself and pray unto HIM. The fire department teaches that we must '*stop, drop and roll'* and I believe we must do that spiritually as well. Stop what you are doing and get down in a position of humility and let your words roll off of your tongue in constant prayer and communication with your Father in heaven.

The Samsonite Marriage: A 40-Day Guide to God's Greatness in Your Relationship

The Bible says that it's 'the little foxes that spoil the vine" and those foxes will ultimately destroy the fruit of your labor. There are many instances where a spouse will just agree to an offer or resolution without fully considering the consequences by consulting God. It is not good to give in or compromise prior to understanding the totality of the problem at hand because it will lead to bitterness or the 'I told you so' moment. It doesn't matter if it is a large purchase such as buying a car or deciding who cooks dinner or who handles certain household duties, there needs to be communication which leads to unity and power.

Reflection:

- I encourage every spouse to remember a decision that you made without consulting your spouse.
- Analyze why you chose to make the decision by yourself.
- How did you and your spouse feel about not having unity in the decision-making process?
- What would you change about the process that you used to reach a decision?

Point of reference scripture:

"Abraham took the wood of the burnt offering and laid it on Isaac his son, and he took in his hand the fire and the knife. So the two of them walked on together." Genesis 22:6 NASB

"Behold, how good and how pleasant it is For brothers to dwell together in unity!" Psalms 133:1 NASB

"Take us the foxes, the little foxes, that spoil the vines: for our vines have tender grapes." Song of Solomon 2:15 KJV

With love always,
Pastors Mike & Mariam Brown

Day 23: **The Power of Absolute Certainty**

Now the angel of the LORD did not appear to Manoah or his wife again. Then Manoah knew that he was the angel of the LORD. Judges 13:21 NASB

As we venture into our twenty-third day of the study on 'A Samsonite Marriage' I believe that the Lord is revealing the power of absolute certainty in our lives. When you think of the term *'absolute certainty'* it is important to understand that it refers to complete confidence that **ELIMINATES ALL DOUBT IN EVERY AREA OF YOUR LIFE**. After the angel of the Lord departed from the presence of Manoah and his wife, Manoah realized that the angelic force and power was truly from God. A key component to success in your marriage is having complete confidence in the things of God despite what you may experience in the natural realm. There are times when we have doubts about our destiny and questions regarding the quests that we have committed to. When you look at your surroundings you may begin to compare your marriage to other people that you come in contact with. In some cases we compare our spouse to other spouses and oftentimes we have a less than positive outlook on our own marriage.

When God designs a man and a wife for each other, HE sees perfection in the union. Sure there are things that we all can improve on but try highlighting the good and perfect things about your spouse instead of the drawbacks. Rather than saying what they struggle at, spend the bulk of your time speaking of their strengths and acknowledging their achievements. How often can your spouse say that you highlight their strong points and positive attributes? How quickly do you overlook the mistakes that they have made and instead appreciate them for just for their efforts. I often say in my home you *might fail trying BUT you weren't trying to fail'*....

Manoah and his wife never argued about the angel leaving and they weren't bitter at eachother during this challenging time in their life. There are many instances where we only miss a good thing when it is gone. It is important to protect and polish our marriages by using the five love languages which are implementing positive words of affirmation when communicating, spending quality time with one another, presenting gifts and tokens of appreciation, performing acts of service to help and assist your spouse. Lastly, doing these four steps will make the fifth love language which is physical touch very easy to engage in. Stay unified with your spouse during the most challenging times in your life and remember **EVERY CHANGE REQUIRES A CHALLENGE!**

Reflection:

- Think about what you say and how you say it to your spouse when youcommunicate.

The Samsonite Marriage: A 40-Day Guide to God's Greatness in Your Relationship

- Ask your spouse to give you feedback on your communication style and skill. Ask your spouse to help you get better in those areas where you can improve?
- Ask your spouse what areas he or she is enjoying in the marriage.

With love always,
Pastors Mike & Mariam Brown

Day 24: Clothing the Naked Eye

"We are doomed to die!" he said to his wife. "We have seen God!" Judges 13:22 NIV

The 24th day of our study brings us to a very crucial point in The Samsonite Marriage and that is *'clothing the naked eye'* which is to have your vision covered in faith. Your eye is one of the most important members of your body because it represents the link between the seen and the unseen. Your eye captures images in the natural realm that are supernatural manifestations of thoughts, ideas and imaginations. At the sight of seeing the presence of God, Manoah immediately feared that he and his wife were doomed to die and soon after he began to speak with the voice of fear. In marriage I recommend discussing the various images that both your natural and spiritual eye captures because it will have a major impact on what your mouth says and how your body moves. Manoah became fearful and it metastasized, which is to spread with an intent to injure, to his mouth and eventually it hindered his movement towards destiny.

Husband and wives are to monitor the impressions that your environment has on you. Our daily experiences have a tremendously powerful impact on our lives due to the fact that we react to our surroundings. When you walk with God your eye is the beholder of beauty and you determine your destiny when you visualize success. When you look too long, at other marriages and what they have or not have it will begin to cloud your vision. Never focus on things outside of your marriage that can potentially hinder your life. Examples of this would be marital issues that your friends and family may be enduring. When you go to work you often communicate with other married individuals about their relationships and those conversations may end up draining your energy or hampering your outlook on your own home.

There are instances when men and women complain about their spouses to others, it fills the air with negativity. That negative information creates images in your mind that are very difficult to delete. Spend time looking at healthy solutions to the unhealthy relationships that you may encounter. Seek remedies and healing agents that can help in resolving issues that may arise so you do not begin to see failure in your life. Delete all detrimental and damaging images from your mind and begin to capture new visions that create positive, lasting sights filled with success.

Reflection:

- Create a list of positive images that you've seen regarding marriage in your day and discuss it with your spouse.
- Create a list of negative images that you have seen regarding marriage. These can be arguments or fights or even divorce commercials that have made some kind of impression in your mind.

Additional Scripture Reference: *"Your eye is the lamp of your body. When your eyes are healthy, your whole body also is full of light. But when they are unhealthy, your body also is full of darkness." Luke 11:34 NIV*

With love always,
Pastors Mike & Mariam Brown

The Samsonite Marriage: A 40-Day Guide to God's Greatness in Your Relationship

Day 25: **Breathing Life #CPR**

"We are doomed to die!" he said to his wife. "We have seen God!" But his wife answered, "If the Lord had meant to kill us, he would not have accepted a burnt offering and grain offering from our hands, nor shown us all these things or now told us this." Judges 13:22-23 NIV

Our 25th day is a continuation of sorts of the previous day's study in that we see the voice of fear being silenced by the voice of love that silences the foolish. Manoah was afraid because he and wife felt the presence of the Lord which made him overreact and think that death was imminent. Manoah's wife played an amazing role by using the power in her tongue according to Proverbs 18:21 to rebuke the spirit of death that came upon her husband.

In a marriage, there are times when your spouse is weakened and becomes physically, emotionally and spiritually fatigued and you are the ONLY ONE that has been predestined to command life to RE enter their body. With the purpose of God in mind, your voice can be perfected as an instrument that performs supernatural C.P.R. on your spouse. Manoah's wife immediately recognized that her husband became fearful because at that time the presence of God in a land full of disobedience represented judgment. When God judged rebellious people, like the children of Israel in Judges 11:1, there would be the extinction of a whole city as punishment. There was a real fear that Manoah and his wife could become as Sodom and Gomorrah, which was totally destroyed by fire. Manoah's wife rebuked the spirit of death by reassuring her husband that God's purpose is not to kill but to bring life more abundantly. Stay focused on resisting the urge to allow someone else's fears follow you until your faith begins to flounder.

God blew HIS breath into each spouse and it is your duty to blow life back into your relationship when you notice fear creeping in. The intention of sin is to kill, so it is very important that you highlight faith over fear, because sin is unbelief that leads to fearful thoughts of torment. Many times people have marital issues such as verbal or physical abuse, sexual indiscretions and adulterous ways that cause couples to become fearful to forgive. The shame of being abused, the hurt of finding out that your spouse has been emotionally or physically unfaithful can be traumatic and devastating. These issues are very serious and they need immediate prayer, fasting and counseling but another danger is it also leads to the erosion of trust. Manoah's wife confronted the spirit of fear that her spouse displayed and acted as a powerful helpmate in the preservation of the marriage.

If you or your spouse has been overtaken by fear and has made a mistake in the marriage, it is important to rebuke the fear to forgive. Without forgiveness, the spirit of death will surely infiltrate your marriage because forgiveness brings new life through reconciliationof that which was separated.

Lastly, Manoah's wife never looked at her husband as a weak man, even though he was having a moment of weakness. She did not question his leadership or authority because she was focused on the will of God due to her personal relationship with the Lord. She spoke of God honoring their offering during their time of need and that is an example of why couples should present their tithes and offerings together as a unified demonstrationof faith. If one spouse is tithing but the other only gives an offering, that house is not as unified as God would have it. Manoah's wife also knew that God would not speak the promises over their lives only to let them die prematurely. You are to know God for yourself and the BREATH of life into your spouse during moments of weakness. REmember, you are not weak because you have a moment of weakness!

Also refer to these scriptures:

Speaking with Strength
"That is why, for Christ's sake, I delight in weaknesses, in insults, in hardships, in persecutions, in difficulties. For when I am weak, then I am strong." 2 Corinthians 12:10 NIV

Knowing God's Gifts
"For God hath not given us the spirit of fear; but of power, and of love, and of a sound mind. Be not thou therefore ashamed of the testimony of our Lord, nor of me his prisoner: but be thou partaker of the afflictions of the gospel according to the power of God;" 2 Timothy 1:7-8 KJV

Breathing Life (CPR)
"And the Lord God formed man of the dust of the ground, and breathed into his nostrils the breath of life; and man became a living soul." Genesis 2:7 KJV

If you have just been added to the study and would like Day 1 through current please feel free to email me and I will forward it to you.

With love always,
Pastors Mike & Mariam Brown

Day 26: **Born Blessed**

And the woman bare a son, and called his name Samson: and the child grew, and the Lord blessed him. Judges 13:24

As the journey continues it has truly been a blessing studying what many of the characteristics of *The Samsonite Marriage*. The 26th day brings us to the birth of Samsonso our topic of the day will be *'**born blessed.'*** The Lord began a mighty work in the lives of Manoah and his wife despite the disobedience that was within the land. The children of Israel continued to disobey God, however, provisions were still being made for the deliverance of the people of God. It is paramount that every marriage has a keen understanding that despite what is going on around you, the Lord, our God has a plan for your deliverance.

Samson's mother was **faithful** to the word of God, she **honored** her husband and she constantly put her flesh under subjection by **living a fasted lifestyle** according to the instructions provided by the angel of the Lord. Manoah was a **humble** man that **feared God** and **loved his wife as he loved himself**. He was a man of **prayer** that **offered his best blessings to God** and was a **leader, at the head of his wife,** by his **obedience** to the things of God, while they remained in **consistent communication** with each other regarding their destiny.

To sum it up, Manoah and his wife **provided an anointed atmosphere** for Samson, to which we can now see that he, Samson, was BORN BLESSED. When you hear someone is *born blessed* oftentimes one may think of the *'silver spoon concept'* which is someone inheriting their riches or status from someone else without having to earn the fame or fortune. On the contrary, Samson inherited one of the greatest challenges EVER which was to deliver a disobedient people, from the hand of a generational enemy that God allowed to rule. To obtain your promise from God there are many characteristics of biblical manhood/womanhood found in the book of Titus chapters 1 & 2 that are to be studied by every Christian couple. Samson was **born blessed** by God yet his parents had to fulfill the call of God on their lives to usher in this great deliverer of the people, which was their very own son.

In your marriage, there are going to be many challenges that you will experience but you must know that you were *born blessed*. You and your spouse were called to birth out greatness in your children, your business, your career and especially the ministry work of the Lord. You may be faced with humbling yourself to avoid an argument that can cause division in your home or forgiving the daily trials that come with learning to be one flesh, but you are to stay focused knowing that deliverance is about to be birthed out of your loins. Challenges may come but change will occur when you remain faithful to the call placed upon your marriage.

Exercises in Excellence:

- Make a list of the ways that you have been blessed by God.
- What characteristics have you displayed over the course of your life that people say are ablessing to their lives? Document it.
- What challenges have you faced that were difficult to overcome in your life and inyour marriage? Write them down and discuss them.

Notice any patterns? Anything that is keeping you from being or feeling blessed? These are the areas you can ask the Almighty to make you better. *Side Note*: To those readerswho are divorced or in transition; these steps are extremely important to discern the misdirection of your past and to help guide the direction of your future.

Additional Scripture Reference:

#BornBlessed: Jeremiah 1:4-5 (KJV)
Then the word of the Lord came unto me, saying, before I formed thee in the belly I knew thee; and before thou camest forth out of the womb I sanctified thee, and I ordained theea prophet unto the nations.

#Biblical Manhood/Womanhood: Titus 2:1-5 (KJV)
But speak thou the things which become sound doctrine: that the aged men be sober, grave, temperate, sound in

faith, in charity, in patience. The aged women likewise, that they be in behavior as becometh holiness, not false accusers, not given to much wine, teachers of good things; that they may teach the young women to be sober, to love theirhusbands, to love their children, to be discreet, chaste, keepers at home, good, obedient to their own husbands, that the word of God be not blasphemed. If you have been added to this study and would like the beginning to current, please feel free to send me a message and I will gladly forward the previous days to you.

YOU WERE BORN BLESSED! Your deliverance is only a few faithful footsteps away. Afew powerful character traits were displayed by Manoah and his wife that allowed the promise of God to be unhindered in their life, among which were: *honor, humility, faithfulness and an undying love and commitment to God and their purpose.* We look forward to your feedback, and we hope you are enjoying the lessons.

With love always,
Pastors Mike & Mariam Brown

The Samsonite Marriage: A 40-Day Guide to God's Greatness in Your Relationship

Day 27: The Sea of Forgetfulness – Micah 7:19

My fears were drowned in PERFECT LOVE
"No longer slaves" Eddie James

Reflection Day

Day 28: Moving by the Spirit During Times of Transition

"And the Spirit of the Lord began to stir him while he was in Mahaneh Dan, between Zorah and Eshtaol." Judges 13:25

As we take a look at our day 28 text, Pastor Mariam and I truly hope that you are being blessed by the daily messages. We are at the midway point of the study and we encourage you to continue with us on this journey into a Samsonite Marriage. Today will examine the movement of the spirit of God that dwelled in Samson.

The Bible says that while Samson was between the two cities of Zorah and Eshtaol the spirit of God began to stir Samson up and this is a very powerful point in that God works while we are in transition. As you look at what a godly marriage should be it is paramount to examine where you currently are and how God is positioning you to prosper. The Lord has put marriages together to be an unbroken fellowship of eternal love for one another in this earthly realm yet there are things that cause separation and division in the union. Marriages are under attack by the enemy, who uses our shortcomings, mistakes and faults against us by making those aforementioned idiosyncrasies seem intentional.

Pay close attention to how you transition from small misunderstandings into full blown arguments and begin to search for patterns and key indicators triggering the explosion. Many things that we argue about as couples are truly minuscule but they are magnified when they are ignored and overlook. Things get overlooked when we downplay them as 'not that serious' when in reality the littlest foxes ruin the vines. Try and talk about every issue before it becomes too burdensome to handle. Encourage communication on all of the obvious areas within your marriage to avoid being negligence

The adversary accuses us and causes constant infighting to destroy the unity of the husband and the wife. Whether it is a toilet seat being left up or a scarf laying lying on an unmade bed, the enemy wants us to argue and be in consistent disagreement with our spouse. Manoah and his wife watched what they prayed for, get birthed out, in the form of Samson as he began to be used while in transition. Samson began to feel the spirit of God move in his life as he was moving from one place to the next. You should look for signs of growth and change in your marriage on a daily basis. Begin to examine how long it takes you to encourage and acknowledge the great qualities that your spouse displays.

When you see your spouse doing things that you like to see, express your appreciation as it will help their mind transition into focusing on doing those good behaviors more and more. The more that you read the word of God, you should be able to quickly transition from anger to love, peace and harmony according to the BEAtitudes in Matthew 5. Married couples should excitedly watch what they've birthed out be moved by the spirit of God. You are not joined together as one to miscarry or abort what The Lord has impregnated you wife. Your husband or wife is to be a partner in the promises of God that are to be made known to the world, so you are to study all transitional words, thoughts and deeds to effectuate perfection in your marriage.

Reflection:

- How long does it take you to recognize positive behaviors in your relationship?
- How long are you upset or bothered by things that your spouse has done?
- How long do you feel they may be affected by something that YOU HAVE DONE? Lol… you make mistakes too!
- How long before you and your spouse jointly repent and reconcile?
- Who is usually the initiator of the reconciliation, and why?

With love always,
Pastors Mike & Mariam Brown

Day 29: **A Recap: (Days 1- 28)**

We have come a little past the midway point in our 45-day journey into Judges 13-14. In our study, we have been taking a divine look at 'The Samsonite Marriage.' Marriage is a unified covenant that God has ordained and we have seen just how we, as the people of God, are to come together to ensure growth and prosperity of that union.

During this learning process, we have come across multiple challenges and blessings that are helping to build and sustain godly marriages and relationships. Topics such as unforgiveness and barrenness have been some key focal points to viewing your relationship differently. Having a spiritual connection with heaven and a strong connection with a spiritual advisor place poignant and powerful messages in your mind that will REdefine your destiny.

Understanding that in order to be perfected by God we must be disciplined in areas of fasting, praying, and studying the Word of God which allows us to have an ear to hear from the Lord. These disciplines also create an atmosphere in which we are able to submit yourselves one to another and acknowledge the hindrances that may be manifesting themselves in the covenant relationship. This will then lead us into the desire to preserve the information downloaded into our spirits REminding us of the promises God has spoken over our lives and activating our Faith to propel us into victory.

We are then moved forward to receive a key element known as covenant communication. Covenant communication is the willingness and desire to seek out our spouse to talk about every detail of our lives. Leaving no stone unturned especially after having heavenly talks with our Father. This also propels us forward to begin to communicate with God together with meekness and humility while removing fear from the marriage. One of the hardest tasks we may be given is to follow the instructions of the Lord so that we may be fruitful in all areas of our lives. This goes back to being disciplined and understanding that following the instructions given are there to help produce a healthy marriage. You are what you eat and following a strict diet of prayer, fasting and studying the Word yields a healthier you as well as a healthier marriage.

There is a continuous flow that moves us into walking in love and peace within the boundaries of the covenant relationship. We learned about hearing what our mate has to say so that we may be able to heal areas of our marriage that have cracks and leaks. Those cracks and leaks have to be sealed to prevent the structural foundation from falling. Sustaining the magnetic pull in marriage by learning and understanding the love language spoken by our spouse helps to seal those areas and keep the enemy from maneuvering his way into the marriage.

The Samsonite Marriage: A 40-Day Guide to God's Greatness in Your Relationship

We are pressed into understanding how to let a leader lead and recognizing godly authority. Paul gives a structural design of the home by showing the man's authority or leadership in the home is based upon his submission to God's ultimate authority and being able to imitate Christ in his actions. This in turns leads us into REpeating the blessed attributes of our spouse which opens our vision to the rewards from God.

We find ourselves meeting and understanding the nature of a #Power Couple. A power couple has learned to operate in unity without the massive breakdowns of selfish gain. They are working to serve God and His people in a capacity that will to draw others untothe Father. Instead of operating in the fleshly realm to solve a spiritual circumstance, they begin to lean towards the spiritual realm to remove fear and doubt. A power couple also utilizes the lessons in the Beatitudes found in Matthew 5 to build a sustainable foundation.

"Rejoicing in hope; patient in tribulation; continuing instant in prayer. (Romans 12:12 KJV)" Here we find three components to implementing a problem-solving strategy. Rejoicing in hope: REminds you that no matter what it looks like a firm faith in God giveshope. Patient in tribulation: REminds us to hold on and not give into the fear and frustration. Have the fruit of patience to endure the trial. Continuing instant in prayer: REminds us to pray right away. Don't try to work things in your own understanding but take it to the Lord immediately.

One of the goals in operating in a unified covenant relationship is to be pleasing in God's sight. We are to present ourselves, the way we live and our relationship as a pure sacrifice to God. Any area in our past that needs to be relinquished must be done so immediately. Genesis 2:24-26 makes known that we are to leave the past behind and cleave unto the future, which is the covenant we vowed before God and our spouse.
This unified stance provokes a divine response from heaven.

In unification, we must begin to operate with absolute certainty, ELIMINATING ALL AREAS OF DOUBT IN OUR LIVES. In essence, it means that we need to remove negative thoughts regarding our spouse and begin to POLISH the positive attributes to encourage confidence. This confidence will allow you both to cover your vision in faith instead of fleshly deceit. It will also help you to perform spiritual CPR on your spouse to revive the areas you may have believed to be barren or even dead.

After all of this REmember, you were BORN BLESSED. You were born with greatness in your DNA to fulfill the works of the LORD. No matter what it looks like or feels like YOU WERE BORN BLESSED. Keep this as a constant reminder so that as you move into a transitional state you can begin to REcall God's movement within your marriage.

The Samsonite Marriage: A 40-Day Guide to God's Greatness in Your Relationship

My prayer is that each person reading the lessons are gleaning some understanding and preparing for the change as well as the challenge that comes from having a new revelation that will create a new reality. God Bless You!

With love always,
Pastors Mike & Mariam Brown

Day 30: **Beauty Blinds Logic**

"And Samson went down to Timnah, and saw a woman in Timnah of the daughters of the Philistines." Judges 14:1 KJV

As we embark on this thirtieth day of our study in the 13th and 14th chapters in the book of Judges there will be a great focus on the Samsonite Marriage through the eyes of the born and the blessed man named Samson. Pastor Mariam and I would love to get your feedback and if you have any questions please feel free to reach out to us.

Our topic for the text is *'beauty blinds logic'* and what that means is your eyes have an *'X-ray like'* ability to pierce through seemingly impenetrable logistic thinking to discover beauty that is buried beneath the surface. Even though Samson was born to be blessed and was destined to achieve greatness he took great risks while reaching for realms beyond imagination. Samson saw a woman, who was of the Philistines camp which was a generational giant that fought against the children of Israel. In a marriage it is important to acknowledge that you are joined together to birth out a fearless fruit of your union.

You will face many issues, problems, situations and circumstances that have systematically stalled your success and you will need to face every obstacle head on without being headstrong. To be headstrong is to be stubborn and self-willed and that character trait leads to instability in the communication patterns of your marriage.

The Samsonite Marriage: A 40-Day Guide to God's Greatness in Your Relationship

Instability leads to the inability! The more that your relationship is defined by inconsistencies within your daily push towards the long term goals you will be susceptible to failure. The Lord should be guiding every individual within the covenant relationship therefore your marriage is to embody a measure of faithfulness that breeds spiritual fearlessness!

Samson ventured into the enemies territory and found beauty that blinded his logic, in that he was to conquer the Philistines, instead he read between the lines of the destiny that God laid out for him. There are many times that a marriage will be faced with the challenge of reading between the blurred lines of life to comprehend the course that the Lord has carved out for couples to follow. Learning forgiveness is a very challenging duty that tons of couples struggle with because very little teaching on reconciliation occurs prior to jumping the broom.

Couples are shell-shocked when faced with the arduous task of forgiving offenses, whether they've committed them or offenses were committed against them. Secondly, forgetting offenses requires couples to constantly REinforce their individual unwillingness to remember the hurt caused by offenses. You are to resist the temptation to remember how hurt you've been or who've you have been hurting and focus on REdefining your understanding of the purpose placed on your marriage. God has planned for marriages to be fruitful and multiply bountifully. Manoah and his wife watched as Samson went fearlessly into hostile territory in pursuit of his purpose. I challenge every person reading this message to fearlessly fight for your future to forge greatness out of grave situations. Your marriage may be in an unfamiliar territory that requires you to think in unconventional ways to achieve uncommon success so it will be your duty to find beauty that blinds logicand reasoning.

Reflection:

- Find areas in your marriage that lacked beauty according to the natural eye.
- How did you overcome the ugliness in the unknown territory?
- What area could you be more fearless in regards to your marriage?
- What areas have do you feel that you have faced your biggest fears?

With love always,
Pastors Mike & Mariam Brown

Day 31: **Crucial Conflict**

"And he came up, and told his father and his mother, and said, I have seen a woman in Timnah of the daughters of the Philistines: now, therefore get her for me to wife." Judges 14:2 KJV

On this 31st day, we find that there is a major issue that arises in those living in *'A Samsonite Marriage'* which points us to the notion that in every relationship there is a *'crucial conflict'* that is necessary for growth. There is a Hip-Hop group named Crucial Conflict and they had an album named *Good Side, Bad Side* and it points to the ebb and flow of life with all of the twists and turns that we will find ourselves going through. Manoah and his wife were faced with a choice that was challenging the charted course that their covenant would take. Samson became infatuated with the woman from the Philistines camp and that decision, one could say should not have been the first option. However, the decision presented Manoah and his wife, with a crucial conflict to their own destiny because he has found a woman that was the offspring of an enemy.

In the bible, the Philistines represent a generational and territorial enemy that operates in familiar ways to destroy the destiny of God's children and Samson has taken a liking to the thing that has plagued the progress of the people of God. Unfathomably, Samson put his parents in between a rock and a hard place by asking them to bring this strange woman to meet him. Samson was arranging the most famous blind date ever!!! Samson's request, however, was a crucial conflict being used by an Almighty God to conquer the enemies of the kingdom of God.

In every marriage, there will be crucial conflicts that have the ability to manifest the miraculous that will ultimately solidify your faith. Be mindful that every conflict in your marriage may not be crucial to your growth and progress. In fact, many of the issues in your marriage are minor circumstances that disrupt the forward progress and lead to stagnation. There is potential for daily disputes to turn into disruptions that will become malignant if there is no discussion on how to confine and defeat the enemy. As you meditate on this text stay focused on what conflicts are crucial to God for your growth.

Reflection:

- Find specific conflicts that you have noticed that have hindered you and yourspouse.
- Find areas that you have grown in your relationship and what conflicts have youovercome during that growth period.
- Locate an area of conflict that you have been concerned with in your life.

The Samsonite Marriage: A 40-Day Guide to God's Greatness in Your Relationship

- Be careful when choosing which battles you fight and engage, because winning every battle does not mean that you will win this spiritual war.
- Avoid random thoughts and ideas that produce negativity and confusion within your life that is not producing positive results in your marriage.

We are nearing the end of our study, and we hope that you are being strengthened and edified by our time in the book of Judges. We look forward to any of your questions, or comments.

With love always,
Pastors Mike & Mariam Brown

Day 32: **Obviously Omitted**

Then his father and his mother said to him, "Is there no woman among the daughters of your relatives, or among all our people, that you go to take a wife from the uncircumcised Philistines?" But Samson said to his father, "Get her for me, for she looks good to me." Judges 14:3 NASB

In this wonderful walk through the book of Judges we are experiencing a myriad of majestic moments that magnify the name of the Lord by way of a godly marriage. As you have chosen to embark on this trek with us, you are encouraged to provide feedback, ask questions and provoke thought with your own perspective of the text. It is our hope that these messages find you well and that you are blessed by the word of the Lord. Our text will be broken down into sections over the next two days with today's focus being on the '*only illogical decision to be made.*'

In marriage there are many opportunities where couples will have to make life altering, mind-blowing selections on their future based on their past and present circumstances. Samson was no different in that he became quickly enamored with the enemies offspring and his parents began to challenge him because he *obviously omitted* the easy choice. Every relationship will be faced with areas that will require problem-solving skills and internal negotiations to reach a common goal yet still there may be some obvious answers being omitted.

The Samsonite Marriage: A 40-Day Guide to God's Greatness in Your Relationship

Samson's parents struggled with the idea that their son found no attraction or appeal to the common choice of a woman being free in a familiar place. Instead Samson sought after a strange woman and his parents provided a level of spiritual rebuke regarding the potential wife. Plainly stated Samson seemed crazy selecting a Philistine woman. Think of times where you had to make a difficult choice, in your marriage that seems obviously wrong and yet because you may have been riddled with bullets of unbelief you ended up questioning your quest for truth.

Too many times we realize that we have compromised our standards of life, marriage and covenant, to compromise with the life of this world that has no true definable traits pointing to prosperity. Like Samson, people of God are too fond of things that do not agree with the predestined path of the righteous. We enjoyed sinful relationships and we embraced ungodliness but as a result we become unproductive in our walk with God. Samson chose the *obvious omission, which* was a woman from a strange land until his mother and father questioned his sight and outlook on who he would be enjoined to marry. Never let your situation determine your salvation in that it may be negatively altering the destiny of the marriage.

I encourage my sisters and brothers reading this to examine the most difficult. You will find some of the most challenging choices that you or your spouse has experienced andhow it has been processed was all wrong. Samson's parents were looking at every other beautiful and qualified woman who could have gladly partaken of the seat soon to be occupied for the glory of God.

With love always,
Pastors Mike & Mariam Brown

The Samsonite Marriage: A 40-Day Guide to God's Greatness in Your Relationship

Day 33: **Unwavering Wants**

"His father and mother replied, "Isn't there an acceptable woman among your relatives or among all our people? Must you go to the uncircumcised Philistines to get a wife?" But Samson said to his father, "Get her for me. She's the right one for me." Judges 14:3 NIV

It is with great joy that Pastor Mariam and I welcome you into day 33 of our in-depth study of The Samsonite Marriage. We hope that you are enjoying the teaching, reviewing the scriptures and using the tips and exercises in your life. Many of these lessons can be instantly integrated into your way of life to bring about change within the areas that The Lord shown you. Some of the steps will require greater study and increased attention to detail to bring forth progression. Hang in there, don't give up, it's not as hard as it may seem. Remember, every change requires a challenge!

Today's message will focus on the pressure of unwavering wants within a marriage. In our text we find Samson choosing to select a woman, to be his wife, who was from the enemies camp of enemy that he was born to conquer and he had an unwavering want of this particular woman. Samson refused to be denied this woman so much so that he challenged his parents to bring her to him against their better judgment. Samson, being a first born male child risked his honorable status and his destiny because he had an unwavering want of this woman. Let's start this lesson with a few questions.

- Have you ever had an unwavering want in your life that you found extremely difficult to deny?
- Has there be something that you felt that you wanted so bad that it became somewhat of a need?
- Have you ever been unwavering about an issue that it changed the course of your life?

Marriage is about dealing with the unwavering wants to ensure that you are not being led by emotional emptiness, spiritual unrest which lead to desperate decision making. Everything that you want should be found in God and HE is the author and finisher of our faith. The Lord is our Shepherd and we shall not want however we will have to make a conscious decision to be led by HIM at all times.

Our emotions can easily move us away from God and the desired closeness that HE seeks to have with us. When we are too consumed with our wants we can disregard our needs! Too often we find our relationships being built on a set of earthly wants and we are then blinded to beauty of our needs. In your will be faced with tough choices where you may feel that you need something only because the want of it has grown so great.

The Samsonite Marriage: A 40-Day Guide to God's Greatness in Your Relationship

Whether it is a want of a new house or a car or even a new job, we must be careful about having deal-breakers and ultimatums that decide our level of joy and happiness. Manoah and his wife struggled with Samson's unwavering want of this daughter of the Philistine camp.

When faced with an unwavering want it is paramount that you and your spouse go back to the basics and communicate your love for one a another which creates unity and produces power in the union. Never forget that your marriage was put together by God before you and your spouse were born, which means HE knows exactly what you need and HE is less moved by what you want.

In closing, having unwavering wants can cause division in your home, which leads to strife and confusion within the marriage. Constantly communicate with your spouse regarding the destiny of your marriage. You were born to be blessed in your covenant status therefore your needs should override your wants.

With love always,
Pastors Mike & Mariam Brown

Day 34: **Window of Opportunity**

His father and mother replied, "Isn't there an acceptable woman among your relatives or among all our people? Must you go to the uncircumcised Philistines to get a wife?" But Samson said to his father, "Get her for me. She's the right one for me." (His parents did not know that this was from the Lord, who was seeking an occasion to confront the Philistines; for at that time they were ruling over Israel.) Judges 14:3-4 NIV

What a wonderful delight it is to have you join us for our miraculous 34th day of the book of Judges. Pastor Mariam and I are learning the great importance of marriage within the ministry of God that has predestined us to have dominion over the earth and multiply within it. We strongly encourage you to take your time to partake in this daily study and feel free to provide your feedback to us.

As part of our topic today, we will examine how God is always looking for a *window of opportunity* to pour out a blessing into our lives that our respective storehouses cannot contain. *The Samsonite Marriage* is one that will be prepared to seize the moment that success and victory hang in the balance as opportunity knocks.

To quickly recap day 33, we learned that Samson sought a woman from the enemy's camp and his parents were conflicted because this decision contradicted their covenant relationship with God. Samson's choice in the Philistine woman was actually a unique *window of opportunity* for God to bring victory to the children of Israel against a generational giant in the Philistines. Many marriages have a lot of obstacles that are in opposition to the purpose and plans that God has for a husband and wife but these goals can be derailed by the enemy. There are special times that we must be on one accord as a family unit to allow the will of God to come alive in a marriage. Samson was being led by an *'all-knowing'* God that watched the enemy torment HIS people for years and this was the perfect time to gain ground on the adversary. In a marriage, certain aspects are crucial turning points that can determine your destiny when those decisions are orchestrated by the Lord. It is important that your relationship remains centered on God and that HE orders your steps just as Samson was being used to bring down the army of the enemy.

In your relationship, you and your spouse will face positions that seem counterproductive to where God is taking you, however, you are to redirect your energy and focus on the will of God. Samson's decision made his parents uncomfortable and you will indeed find this new walk conflicting with your future because your choices will confront areas that you may have compromised in the past.

In closing, it is a challenging thing to remain in the face of God with all of the distractions that the world tempts us with. Samson had a strong relationship with God, who promised that he would be a mighty king, and he was directed by the Lord to do the unbelievable thing which was to commit to marrying the uncommon woman. Take advantage of the *window of opportunity* that is right before your eyes and seize the moment until you obtain victory.

With love always,
Pastors Mike & Mariam Brown

Day 35: **Ready for the Roar**

"Then went Samson down, and his father and his mother, to Timnah, and came to the vineyards of Timnah: and, behold, a young lion roared against him." Judges 14:5 KJV

In today's segment of A Samsonite Marriage, we will tackle the topic of couples being ready for the roar of the lion seeking to devour what you have raised. Samson went through the town of Timnah looking for the woman that God sent him to find and he and his parents were met by a lion that roared against them.

On the road to your destiny there will be opposing forces strategically aligned in your path to deter you. These obstacles may come in the form of layoffs, arguments, health issues and marital mistakes and mishaps that the enemy uses to separate what God has put together. Scripture leads us towards being steadfast and unmovable in the face of a crisisknowing that Christ is still with you.

In the book of Isaiah chapter 9 it says that Emmanuel is our *'Wonderful Counselor'* who will guide us through our darkest moments and will lead us into the marvelous light. The enemy of your soul hates marriage because it represents the reproduction of the prototype of God's greatness; therefore, he stalks us waiting for an opportunity to devourour destiny. It may be a challenge to walk in love and forgiveness but the foregoing of these fruits of the spirit will leave a deep-rooted seed of bitterness that leaves a sour taste in your mouth. Your mouth is a major vessel of valor that is able to bring forth victory by using the power of your tongue, which controls life and death. I recommend that you seek God both as individuals and as a couple to help your union be prepared for the roaring lion that will attempt to cause fear, doubt and torment through various trials, tribulations and trauma. One may ask how can I be ready when the lion begins to roar?

In the second chapter of the book of Acts, Paul provides four steps to help us stay on guard beginning in verse 42: remaining dedicated to the teaching; finding fellowship; breaking bread; and prayer.

In closing, meditating on the word of God both day and night will allow you to have a unabated focus on living a life pleasing to the Lord and one that enhances your experiences with others. Your marriage is to be equipped with the proper tools to build a wonderful, long lasting godly covenant.

The Samsonite Marriage: A 40-Day Guide to God's Greatness in Your Relationship

Additional Scripture Reference:

Being Ready: *"Be sober, be vigilant; because your adversary the devil, as a roaring lion, walketh about, seeking whom he may devour:"* 1 Peter 5:8 KJV

Mediation on the word: *"But his delight is in the law of the Lord; and in his law doth he meditate day and night."* Psalms 1:2 KJV

Using the power of the WORD: *"Death and life are in the power of the tongue: and they that love it shall eat the fruit thereof."* Proverbs 18:21 KJV

With love always,
Pastor Michael & Mariam Brown

Day 36: **The Spirit of the Lord. It's on You!**

"And the Spirit of the Lord came mightily upon him, and he rent him as he would have rent a kid, and he had nothing in his hand: but he told not his father or his mother what he had done." Judges 14:6 KJV

Good day to you from Pastor Mariam and I. We pray that you are enjoying your day in Jesus name. We know that life may be very hectic and it is hard to find time for yourself but it is with thanks that you have chosen to read this message today and we hope that itfinds you well! We know that everyone that reads this 45th day of study is not married in the natural but all if you are married to something albeit your dreams, goals, careers and most importantly you are married to the Lord. This study will help you in every area of your life as it has basic principles that can literally be applied to any area of your existence.

As we dive into our 36th day we are met with the introduction of the spirit of the Lord as it comes upon Samson in a time of need. Your life was not made to be filled with luck, chance and randomness in regards to success, joy, love, peace and happiness!!
You were designed for divine favor and you were preordained to prosper.

When faced with a random attack from a roaring lion Samson felt the power of God come upon his life and he ripped the attacking animal to shreds!!!!! Like Samson, you were bornto be filled with the spirit of the Lord, so in times of trouble, uncertainty, fear and famine,HE, the LORD can be your present help according to Psalm 46.

Every marriage faces challenges like miscommunications, misconceptions and even misconduct but the Lord provides the power to overcome those situations by **HIS LOVE**. In Proverbs 10:12 it says, "Hatred stirreth up strifes: but love covereth all sins" which means that some things will be stirred up **BUT LOVE IS THE DECIDING FACTOR TO YOUR VICTORY**.

Pastor Mariam and I are approached all the time with similar issues in marriages and relationships that have one common struggle and that is a lack of communication. Men often say *'she doesn't understand me'* or *'I cannot get her to respect me'* and women feel that *'he is not leading me'* and *'he is talking and I cannot read his mind'* so there's **CONFUSION IN THE COVENANT**!!! Avoid allowing these blockages in communication to destroy the destiny that God has planned for you. Reconciliation is the key to reaching your destiny in the Lord. Disunity is designed by the devil to destroy the divine plan of God over you and the things that you love. The enemy would love nothing better than to have you forget how to access the spirit of the Lord, the very present help that is available in troubling times.

COMMUNICATION with God is very important during challenging times in life because every answer on earth is found in heaven. The Lord wants you to have a direct connection with HIM at all times. The adversary, satan tries to interrupt your signal with the savior and just like areas with poor cell phone reception or poor Wi-Fi connectivity, satan seeks to block your access to God by causing you to be fearful, which leads to torment and then you are unable to have the mind of Christ. Without being able to think on the things of God, you are prone to overreact and overcompensate which leads to disaster.

In closing, the spirit of the Lord is available at all times and it is an invaluable tool for victory in any challenging situation. Whether you are married in the natural or preparing for marriage you are encouraged to create an atmosphere that is conducive to the Holy Spirit because it provides power over all things that come against you. You can rip apart any attacking lion trying to attach its sharp teeth into your life. You have greatness in yourDNA by the spirit of the Lord that is upon you.

Exercise:

Repeat these affirmations to declare victory over ever roaring lion attacking you:

- The spirit of the Lord is upon me to defeat every attack on my life.

- I am victorious over every vicious and violent enemy seeking to destroy my destiny.
- Whatever I put my hands towards will prosper and I cannot fail or fall short.

Additional Scripture Reference: *"The Lord will send a blessing on your barns and on everything you put your hand to. The Lord your God will bless you in the land he is givingyou."* Deuteronomy 28:8 NIV

With love always,
Pastors Mike & Mariam Brown

Day 37: **Stop, Look & Listen**

"So he went down and talked to the woman; and she looked good to Samson."Judges 14:7 NASB

Our 37th day points us to studying the power of being able to stop, look and listen to the important voices concerning your life. Samson saw a woman who caught his attention and he began to visually connect with her as he felt the power of her words captivate him. There are times in our life when a multitude of things are fighting for our attention and weneed to be able to have a razor-sharp focus on the most important issues at hand.

The Word of God, in the sixth chapter of Matthew focusing on the thirty-third verse, gives a very simple plan to achieving success in any area of your life and that is to keep God first and allow everything else to fight for second place. "But seek ye first the kingdom of God, and his righteousness; and all these things shall be added unto you.(Matthew 6:33 KJV)" Samson had a relationship with God, that was preordained before he was formed in his mother's womb and the moment that he saw the woman from Timnah, he knew thatshe was destined to be his wife

.It was clear to Samson that his attraction to this woman was of God therefore he listenedintently as she spoke. In your life it is very important to have a strong relationship with God, through prayer, fasting and reading HIS written word so that you have a clear view on your purpose.

The Samsonite Marriage: A 40-Day Guide to God's Greatness in Your Relationship

Samson was not looking at the physical characteristics of the woman; instead his curiosity was provoked by the promise spoken over his life by the Lord.

There are many instances where we judge our life and our potential prosperity based on the natural things in life. We look at people's financial status, their career path, their outer looks and even their educational background as a guide to make decisions on love and marriage. You must stop and resist the natural urge to evaluate a relationship that should revolve around covenant and limit it to the convenience of some exterior and superficial standard.

In closing, stop paying attention to the distractions of life and look closely on the places in your life that need to be governed by God. Lastly, listen to the voice of the Lord through prayer as HE guides every step that you take on life.

Reflection:

- Stop and think about how God has blessed you and give HIM thanks wherever you are.

- Look towards the hills whenever you feel overwhelmed or overcome by fear andGod will provide answers to all of your needs.
- Listen to HIS Word and obey it because obedience ushers in the presence of the Lordmore than any sacrificial offering that you could ever present.

With love always,
Pastors Mike & Mariam Brown

The Samsonite Marriage: A 40-Day Guide to God's Greatness in Your Relationship

Day 38: **Turn it Around**

"And after a time he returned to take her, and he turned aside to see the carcass of the lion: and, behold, there was a swarm of bees and honey in the carcass of the lion." Judges 14:8 KJV

Good day to all of our faithful readers of the 40-day study on *The Samsonite Marriage*, we pray that you are blessed beyond measure by the teaching. On this 38th day, The Lord wants us to prosper in everything that we do concerning marriage by communicating a unified love that breeds power in our lives. We challenge you to be strong in the Lord and the power of HIS might.

In life, you are sure to face various trials, tribulations and tests that are tremendously difficult to understand and overcome but remember that God sees your situation and he will *turn it around*. Your marriage is no different in that God has joined you and your spouse to link up in prayer and fasting to break every stronghold off of your life. Samson, saw a woman that appealed to him and he had intentions for her to become his wife however there was one major issue which was Samson had something dead in his way. There are many things in our life that are lifeless, motionless and in fact dead therefore we may have given up on these areas.

The daily pressures of life, such as school, work, church and family, can make it easy to neglect and overlook some marital basics. It's at this point that we need God to help us turn it around in our favor. It is important to take time every day to turn your focus to your spouse by having daily conversations that include words of encouragement, positive reinforcement and uplifting and empowering interactions between husband and wife.

Samson faced the danger of being stung by multiple bees while moving close to the carcass of the lion. In marriage, you will need to get out of your comfort zone and take daily risks to reap long lasting rewards in your relationship. As a husband or a wife, you are the only one responsible to protect and polish your spouse with the love of God. Never leave that responsibility unattended because you will forfeit the fortune and favor that God intended for your life.

Reflection:

- Use your bible to help you find passages on Christ-like behaviors for the husband and wife.
- Create a schedule to encourage your spouse on a daily basis via text messages, phone calls and emails that reinforce love and intimate ideas that are mutually shared.

The Samsonite Marriage: A 40-Day Guide to God's Greatness in Your Relationship

- Reach out for help if you cannot find the most effective ways to create anatmosphere that is filled with communication, unity and power.

In closing, we empower you to take the bull by the horn in your marriage and apply these teachings to bless your covenant. You will see tremendous growth if you remain consistent, committed, obedient and faithful to the goal of God for your marriage. The Lord wants us to prosper in everything that we do concerning marriage by communicating a unified love that breeds power in our lives.

We challenge you to be strong in the Lord and the power

of HIS might. With love always,
Pastors Mike & Mariam Brown

Day 39: **Full Disclosure in Marriage**

"And he took thereof in his hands, and went on eating, and came to his father and mother, and he gave them, and they did eat: but he told not them that he had taken the honey out of the carcass of the lion." Judges 14:9 KJV

God has placed a special place for full disclosure which reflects the commandment to avoid lies, untruths and hidden information to create an atmosphere of oneness through openness. In this 39 day of our study we find Samson bring his father and mother some very precious honey to indulge in but there was not full disclosure on the origin. Samson did not tell his parents where this honey came from. Even though the honey may have been sweet it's origin may have been from a sour place. There are things that arrive and come up in every marriage that have come from unknown places. Marriage is designed for couples to leave all things from their past behind so that they may cleave unto their spouse. A wonderful example of this is found in the book of Ruth, where Boaz expresses his appreciation that Ruth has stepped out of her comfort zone to restart her life.

Every component of Ruth's life was fully disclosed to Boaz and there was nothing hidden from his sight. This is how marriage is to be for each of us. No secrets and no taboos in the tabernacle of the marriage covenant. The origin of a feeling or a thought is very important because the Bible teaches us in James 1:17 that the origin of every perfect giftis from above. God did not give us a spirit of fear but he discloses that HE releases power, love and a sound mind to each of us which helps us be victorious in every difficult situationthat we face.

Eliminating the effects of our past is crucial in the marriage covenant because old issuessuch as undisclosed secrets, thoughts and experiences are potential hindrances to the forward progression of a marriage. God has designed marriage to be about sharing everything by communicating with one another which establishes unity and leads to power within the marriage. It is important to share with one another because you are joint heirs with Christ and each of you has power that will bear amazing results when they areworking in unison.

Reflection:

- Offer your heart to God. Ask HIM to search it so that you may be washed clean.
- Confess your faults and watch as your mutual openness blessed your marriage.

With love always,
Pastors Mike & Mariam Brown

Day 40: **RSVP**

"Then Samson's father accompanied him to Timnah for the marriage. Samson hosted a party there, for this was customary for bridegrooms to do. When the Philistines saw he had no attendants, they gave him thirty groomsmen who kept him company." Judges 14:10-11 NET

We are so happy that you are on this adventure through the scriptures! Relationships are the centerpiece of life and as such, it is important to study how we can preserve the relationships with those that we love. Above all else, we hope that you are encouraged to work through any situations to ensure the health and vitality of all the relationships in your life. We look forward to hearing your feedback and receiving your comments as it relates to these studies.

As we conclude on this 40-day study of the book of Judges 13-14 we are closing the study by taking a look at the life of Samson at the moment that he marries his much sought after bride. This has been a wonderful study and Pastor Mariam and I are very thankful that you have embarked on this journey with us.
Scripture:

Many parties, events, ceremonies and celebrations are

being planned everyday all across the world and almost universally there is an understanding of the acronym 'rsvp' which simply asks the invitee to 'please respond'. The term 'rsvp' is requesting a response to an invitation to confirm one's attendance or presence. Your presence is invaluable!! You are one of a kind and have been predestined for greatness therefore you will attract others that will be intrigued to celebrate your successes in life. In the book of 1st Peter the second chapter tells us that we are a royal priesthood and a chosen generation with special skills and abilities that will be used to be a change-making entity wherever you go. When you walk in a room there should be an aura that arrives with you and it is the spirit of God that is realized by the joy on your face via your smile or the confidence thatyou exude as you interact with others.

Even your enemies can recognize the anointing on your life as you are embarking on new territories and lands that have been previously unattainable. Samson was called by Godwith a prophetic promise on his life before he was born, to change the course of the peoplebased on the will of God that was working within him. Your marriage is surrounded by onlookers, passerby's and hopefuls and skeptics that are watching your every move so itis paramount that you perform with power in every moment. In Judges 14:11, the enemyfeared Samson and sent spies to get close to him to commence his demise. There will always be temptation around you and your marriage that would love nothing more than to separate and destroy what God has put together. Stay focused on your faith in the

Father who sent HIS son with all power in HIS hand to pull every enemy underneath HIS feet. God has preordained your overwhelming success in marriage so by HIS stripes your marriage is blessed and highly favored. Your marriage can never fail if you do not quit as a couple. Be great, be blessed and remember there's greatness in your DNA!

With love always,
Pastors Mike & Mariam Brown

The Samsonite Marriage: A 40-Day Guide to God's Greatness in Your Relationship

About the Authors

Pastor Mike Brown and Pastor Mariam Brown

Isaiah 61:1

The Spirit of the Lord God is upon me, because the Lord has anointed me to bring the good news to the poor: he has sent me to bind up the brokenhearted, to proclaim liberty to the captives, and the opening of the prison to those who are bound.

Serving as joint heirs to the kingdom, Pastor Mike and Pastor Mariam serve God wholeheartedly. God is a covenant keeper and these two individuals show how God honors the covenant of marriage through ministry and teaching. A foundational covenant teaching is Christ relationship with the church.